Regenerating Education as a Living System

BRIDGING THEORY AND PRACTICE

Series Editor: Jeffrey Glantz

Bridging Theory and Practice is an international series on school leadership that reflects the latest cutting-edge theories and practice in school leadership. The series motto is framed after Kurt Lewin's famous statement, paraphrased, that there is no sound theory without practice, and no good practice that is not framed on some theory. Authors in this series illustrate the intimate and integral connection between the two divides.

Books In Series

Regenerating Education as a Living System: Success Stories of Systems Thinking in Action edited by Kristen M. Snyder and Karolyn J. Snyder

Bridging Leadership and School Improvement: Practical Strategies for Improving Teaching and Learning by Leslie Ann Locke and Sonya D. Hayes

Principal Recruitment and Retention: Best Practices for Meeting the Challenges Today edited by Chanina Rabinowitz and Michael Reichel

Actionable Feedback to PK–12 Teachers edited by Alyson L. Lavigne and Mary Lynne Derrington

Systems Thinking for Sustainable Schooling: A Mindshift for Educators to Lead and Achieve Quality Schools edited by Karolyn J. Snyder and Kristen M. Snyder

For a complete list of books in the Bridging Theory and Practice series, please see https://rowman.com/Action/SERIES/_/RLBTP/Bridging-Theory-and-Practice

Regenerating Education as a Living System

Success Stories of Systems Thinking in Action

Edited by

Kristen M. Snyder
Karolyn J. Snyder

ROWMAN & LITTLEFIELD
Lanham • Boulder • New York • London

Published by Rowman & Littlefield
An imprint of The Rowman & Littlefield Publishing Group, Inc.
4501 Forbes Boulevard, Suite 200, Lanham, Maryland 20706
www.rowman.com

86-90 Paul Street, London EC2A 4NE, United Kingdom

Copyright © 2023 by Kristen M. Snyder and Karolyn J. Snyder

All rights reserved. No part of this book may be reproduced in any form or by any electronic or mechanical means, including information storage and retrieval systems, without written permission from the publisher, except by a reviewer who may quote passages in a review.

British Library Cataloguing in Publication Information Available

Library of Congress Cataloging-in-Publication Data

Names: Snyder, Kristen M., 1964- editor. | Snyder, Karolyn J., editor.
Title: Regenerating education as a living system : success stories of systems thinking in action / edited by Kristen M. Snyder, Karolyn J. Snyder.
Description: Lanham, Maryland : Rowman & Littlefield, 2023. | Series: Bridging theory and practice | Includes bibliographical references. | Summary: "The stories in this book offer strategies and practices for applying systems thinking in education to unleash human energy for the journey of continuous improvement"—Provided by publisher.
Identifiers: LCCN 2023017532 (print) | LCCN 2023017533 (ebook) | ISBN 9781475866421 (cloth) | ISBN 9781475866438 (paperback) | ISBN 9781475866445 (epub)
Subjects: LCSH: Educational evaluation. | Educational change. | Educational leadership. | School management and organization.
Classification: LCC LB2822.75 .R439 2023 (print) | LCC LB2822.75 (ebook) | DDC 370—dc23/eng/20230505
LC record available at https://lccn.loc.gov/2023017532
LC ebook record available at https://lccn.loc.gov/2023017533

Contents

Series Editor Foreword	vii
Foreword	ix
Preface	xi
Editors' Introduction	xiii
Chapter 1: Systems Thinking in Curriculum Development in Finland *Irmeli Halinen*	1
Chapter 2: Leadership Preparation for Sustainable Schooling *Michele Acker-Hocevar*	17
Chapter 3: Principal Networking for School Sustainability *Renee Sedlack, David Scanga, Tammy Berryhill, and Claudia Steinacker*	33
Chapter 4: Systems Thinking Training and School District Transformation *John Mann*	47
Chapter 5: Toward a Human Networked School: A Natural Energy System *Karolyn J. Snyder*	63
Chapter 6: The Magic of Esprit de Corps Isn't Really Magic *John Fitzgerald, PhD*	79
Chapter 7: (Re)imagined Teacher Learning and Improvement with Systems Thinking: Corbett Prep and Its "Culture of Fit" *Helen M. Hazi*	95

Chapter 8: Complexity Thinking as a Way of Living to Develop
   Sustainable Schooling   109
   Elaine C. Sullivan and John Fitzgerald

Chapter 9: Storytelling as a Strategic Leadership Tool   123
   Kristen M. Snyder

About the Editors and Contributors   139

Series Editor Foreword

Jeffrey Glanz

A word about the current book in the Bridging Theory and Practice series: *Regenerating Education as a Living System: Success Stories of Systems Thinking in Action*, competently edited by Kristen Snyder and Karolyn Snyder, co-editors of another book in this Series: *Systems Thinking for Sustainable Schooling: A Mindshift for Educators to Lead and Achieve Quality Schools.*

Each chapter in this volume brilliantly discusses a different facet of the topic, and that diversity and depth make this book unique. The editors crafted each chapter logically and intelligently by framing Systems Thinking as curriculum development, leadership preparation, professional networking, professional development, influencing teaching and learning, as a way of life, and as storytelling.

Each chapter is rich in theory yet combined with practical advice as to how to make systems thinking a reality in all schools. Of particular note, is Hazi's chapter that discusses her visit to a school that has implemented, or shall I say, "lives" systems thinking in all its varied facets. The chapter is a must-read for leaders who wish to improve their own schools.

With that said, the book is filled with stories, if you will, on making systems thinking a reality. The cogent and inspiring reflections by each contributor bring systems thinking and related theories alive, doable, and inspiring. The book encourages school leaders to reimagine the school away from a traditional organization. Each contributor, explicitly or implicitly, challenges readers to, in the words of Maxine Greene "find apertures in the wall of what is taken for granted; to pierce the webs of obscurity; to see and then to choose." The greatest contribution of this work, it seems to me, is to stir educational leaders to utilize a systems thinking approach as they go about organizing and running their schools for maximum benefit to students, teachers, parents, administrators, and the community at large.

This book, *Regenerating Education as a Living System: Success Stories of Systems Thinking in Action* combined with its partner book, previously published a few months ago, *Systems Thinking for Sustainable Schooling: A Mindshift for Educators to Lead and Achieve Quality Schools,* offer school leaders and policymakers a recipe, if you will, for what Systems Thinking can do for schools to improve teaching and learning.

All comments may be sent to the individual contributors, co-editors, and, or the Series Editor. We hope this new volume in the Rowman & Littlefield School Leadership will bring fresh ideas to improve our schools.

Foreword

Anneli Rautiainen

Learning is in crisis! Unexpected complex global problems have affected schools everywhere. A system change is needed! Traditional top-down models are inadequate for today's systems-driven learning environments. Therefore, a vital strategy and robust processes are needed to build sustainable systems that are based on communication and dialogue. Organizational learning communities and networks tend to support leadership to sustain quality and innovative cultures within increasing levels of volatility, uncertainty, complexity, and ambiguity.

Despite the reality that systems thinking has been spreading for decades, it has affected leadership and strategic development in education within only a small group of innovators. When the learning environment around us is shaky, people tend to rely on safe old ways of acting and leading, but going back to traditional practices and leadership practices is not the solution. On the contrary, this outdated approach leads to more severe problems concerning teachers' burnout and students' lack of well-being. Both teachers and students start feeling inadequate because the complex problems are not being resolved for them.

The ownership of thinking and acting systemically must become mainstream. We must move from objects to relationships, from measuring to mapping, from quantities to qualities, and from structures to processes. This requires trust that is built by learning together, not knowing the answers beforehand. It is also created by piloting and experimenting with innovations to see what works and what doesn't rather than scaling up a ready-made concept.

The well-known researchers and authors in this book *(Regenerating Education as a Living System: Success Stories of Systems Thinking in Action)* not only describe well the current situation and crisis but also bring new tools, such as storytelling, to strengthen motivation and commitment to build a brighter future for students. Creating space to tell stories helps to translate ideas into action. Simultaneously, human networking is becoming a vital strategy around the world and fostering continuous learning in the learning community.

I highly recommend this book for leaders, practitioners, policymakers, researchers, or anyone interested in working for the future, and for our helping students to solve complex problems such as the worldwide learning crises. Providing equal opportunities for all learners across the globe is our shared responsibility. Now is the time to act!

Preface

Kristen M. Snyder and Karolyn J. Snyder

The story of education is increasingly complex in the 21st century, and some might even say it is chaotic. Stories abound of budget cuts, failing students, teacher shortages, and the exodus of principals from schools. These are among the telling signs that a major problem exists in education. Add to this grim picture the comparisons on international standardized tests that prompt educators in various countries to ponder why their schools are not as good as those in other nations. Yet, stories of leaps in learning and innovation are also emerging that provide hope for creating a new direction in education that is sustainable. This book provides readers with a language based on systems thinking to help them become cocreators in this new story.

Regenerating Education as a Living System: Success Stories of Systems Thinking in Action is the second in a series dedicated to exploring the application of systems thinking in education to contribute to the sustainability of education worldwide. The book is written by educators in the Systems Thinkers in Education Network (STEN) who have been working together in various combinations for over 30 to 50 years, applying systems thinking in practice. Systems Thinking is not new to education. The problem is that the natural laws of physics, which are reflected herein, have not yet been applied or taught across the board.

The title of the book reflects our position that education is a living system embedded in a societal context, interacting with changes in the global landscape. The system of education, at all levels, from the national to the classroom level, is both impacted by and impacts what happens in society. The global landscape is evolving, yet education lags behind. Educators need support to be responsive and adaptive to the changing landscape to ensure that the youth of today are prepared to lead in a sustainable future.

"Regenerating" education is to suggest the need for renewal. In the field of biology, regeneration reflects the growth of new cells or tissues after loss or damage. Education has indeed been damaged by the political agendas of accountability that punish schools rather than support their continuous development. The principalship is in crisis, leaving other levels of educators ill-prepared to respond adequately to the complexity of schooling today. Teachers are burned out from budget cuts and teaching to the test. and students are left on their own to build bridges between classroom learning and living in the real world.

This is a book of hope for educators who are committed to creating learning spaces that prepare children and youth as participants and leaders of a sustainable global future. This is a book of inspiration from stories of educators who have been engaged in systems approaches to educational development for over 50 years. This is a book of concrete examples of how Systems Thinking can be applied at all levels of the education system, from a national curriculum to classroom learning. Join this global collective to regenerate education and build new cells to support the growth of energy systems for sustainability and innovation

Editors' Introduction

Kristen M. Snyder and Karolyn J. Snyder

The language used in education today has a direct impact on the ability to sustain education for the future. The current language of educational leadership is dominated by a focus on governance and accountability systems, student grades, budgets, and personnel issues, which are reinforced by education policy. This focus lacks a long-term vision and a Systemic Approach to leading and developing sustainable educational systems.

As demonstrated in chapter 2, most Principal Preparation programs focus on managing buildings, finances, and personnel, rather than on leading in rapidly changing and complex times, developing teams, and building a culture of participation. Even fewer programs consider what it means to lead educational systems and schools from a quality perspective. As illustrated in chapter 1, this static orientation lacks the dynamics of a Systems Approach, and as history has shown, leaves educators climbing an uphill battle to survive.

Educators need a new language and mindset to create the conditions for sustainable, continuous development in education. Chapters in this book are designed to help readers "unearth" the importance of Systems Thinking and understand its centrality to the sustainability of education as a social system. This book gives readers big ideas about how to think about continuous development that is grounded in Systems Thinking and a language for implementation. The theory of Systems Thinking is explained and concretized through stories of its application at all levels of the educational system.

The stories in this book offer strategies and practices for unleashing human energy for the journey of continuous improvement, which is the essential feature of a Systemic Approach to education systems. Through the stories, a language is communicated about what is Systems Thinking in practice and how it can be organized to support curriculum development and principal preparation. The stories also offer practical tools for designing and sustaining education systems that fit our complex and rapidly changing times.

The first two chapters of the book explore Systems Thinking through stories about the national curriculum development initiatives in Finland and university-level principal preparation programs in the United States. In chapter 3, Network Thinking is presented as a critical component for school districts to sustain school leaders for quality schooling. In chapter 4, readers are guided through a 25-year journey of a school district that implemented Systems Thinking at all levels, from classroom to district-level administration, sharing its impact.

In the fifth chapter, Networking Theory is taken to a whole new level as a management strategy to help leaders design infrastructures that support adaptability and responsiveness in complex systems. Chapter 6 is the story of a turnaround school that was down, recovered over time, and rediscovered its potential through Systems Thinking. In chapter 7, readers go inside a school's culture to explore alternative approaches to teacher evaluation that are designed around a "culture of fit."

In chapter 8, the concept of Complexity Thinking is introduced as a concrete practice when implementing Systems Thinking. In this chapter, readers gain insights into how to reimagine school development and integrate the global context into daily student learning. The final chapter illustrates the power of storytelling as a leadership tool and strategy to develop work cultures that are built on trust, courage, and dialogue to support sustainable quality in education.

As you turn the pages of this book, we hope you are inspired by the big ideas to chart new pathways of thinking and practice for a more sustainable future for education. Perhaps you will find yourself reflecting on your own journey, renewing hidden treasures that can become part of the regeneration of education as a living system. Together, educators can shape a bold new story of *Education as a Sustainable Living System*.

Chapter 1

Systems Thinking in Curriculum Development in Finland

Irmeli Halinen

The purpose of this chapter is to describe how a systems thinking approach is embedded in the education development in Finland, and especially how systems thinking was actualized in extensive national curriculum reform in 2012–2016. These experiences may encourage readers to reflect on the importance of multidimensional interaction, networking and collaboration, and the sustainability of educational changes. The chapter emphasizes the importance of sufficient alignment between the regulators of change at all levels of the education system. Alignment is needed, particularly in large-scale reforms.

For several decades, schooling in Finland has been a system of interconnected agencies to support school learning. The spirit of collaboration and trust has gradually strengthened into a common learning process of various actors. This national, dialogical mindset has paved the way for the most recent curriculum reform, which involved all schools and local education authorities, various organizations, and the whole society. The urgent task was to transform education so that it better promotes meaningful learning and a sustainable way of life as well as contributes to solutions to local and global challenges.

Central in the reform process were the principles of transparency, collaboration, coherence, and sustainability. The reform embodied systems thinking; networking and team intelligence in national curriculum processes; local and school-based processes; and school leadership, teaching, and learning. In Finland, it is important that educators have opportunities to apply systems thinking in practice and develop their own thinking and collaboration skills. This chapter examines how the reform strengthened the prerequisites of municipal and school leaders to lead their schools as living systems and gives practical tools for how to do this.

SYSTEMS APPROACH, NETWORK THINKING, AND QUALITY IN THE FINNISH EDUCATION SYSTEM

The present Finnish education system has been developed coherently during the past 50 years. Looking back at this history, we can see a continuous learning process in which all actors at different levels and dimensions of the system have, step-by-step, developed their skills to interact, negotiate, and collaborate in order to find the best ways to organize education and improve its quality. Teachers and their national union are always involved when changes in the education system or curriculum are planned.

The development path has been a process where the interconnectedness of the various elements of the education system, such as administrative structures, curriculum, assessment system, teacher education, and textbooks, as well as an ongoing dialogue with the surrounding society, has been regarded as vital. Constant efforts have been made to create networks and find consensus, promote system coherence, and get all elements and actors to serve common goals. At the same time, open debate with critical opinions and even contradictory viewpoints has not only been allowed but consciously preferred.

Today, the Finnish education system is an internationally recognized example of a high-performing system that successfully combines high-quality education with equity and social cohesion through reasonable public funding (Niemi et al., 2012). In extensive reforms, financial resources have often been too scarce which has then complicated renewal. Nonetheless, people have learned to look for innovative solutions, which have been possible due to the autonomy of actors and the flexibility of the education system.

Values of equity and equality as well as principles of all-around development and lifelong and life-wide learning have been guiding the development of education (Niemi, 2014). The focus is on learners and their learning and well-being. This approach aims at equipping all learners with competencies needed in the 21st century, including knowledge, awareness, thinking and collaboration, and socio-emotional skills and behaviors.

One of the unique features of the Finnish education system is the ethos of trust. It becomes visible in the functioning and culture of education, and it makes fruitful cooperation and collaboration possible. Besides trusting everybody's possibilities to learn, trust is also evident in the structures of the system. There are hardly any controlling mechanisms such as school inspections or high-stakes testing of students. (Halinen et al., 2016). Instead, municipalities, schools, and teachers have wide autonomy, and student participation is actively developed. Assessment and evaluation are used to promote learning rather than to compare.

CURRICULUM AS A SYSTEMIC AND INTERACTIVE TOOL

Curriculum has a central role in the education system. It is a pedagogical, legal, and administrative tool that creates firm and supportive guidelines for the work of all teachers. In Finland, big reforms in education always include changes in curriculum, and through those reforms, schools and the whole education system progress. A curriculum is like a roadmap that concretizes educational values, goals, and culture as well as a common direction of educational and pedagogical development. It is a compass that leads the way forward and through wide networks influences society.

Today, according to the Education Act, the Finnish curriculum system is formed of two actual layers: a national core curriculum and local, usually municipal, curriculum. These are the obligatory elements. Education providers may also decide that all schools in their area draw up a school-based curriculum, which forms a third layer in the system. In most cases, the local curriculum includes municipal curricular guidelines and school-based curricula.

Local curricula are drawn up according to the guidelines of the national core curriculum, and teachers have wide pedagogical autonomy when they plan teaching and learning processes based on the local curriculum. The curriculum is not only about the content of various subjects but more importantly about the principles of education.

The core curriculum includes main guidelines for values, learning conception, educational goals and main tasks, school culture, support for learning and well-being, and student assessment, as well as the tasks, objectives, core content, and assessment criteria of school subjects. It is a holistic description of high-quality education in a rich and supportive learning environment. Municipal and school-based curricula contextualize national guidelines to local circumstances. They take the needs of students, as well as specific municipal and school features, challenges, and opportunities, into consideration.

The national core curriculum is dependent on the Education Act, which stipulates the main goals for education as well as the obligatory school subjects, and on the government decree, which stipulates the allocation of lesson hours among school subjects. National core curricula for all levels of education (excluding universities) are designed and decided by the Finnish

National Agency for Education, an autonomous and nonpolitical expert office under the auspices of the Ministry of Education and Culture. The ministry has delegated all power concerning the core curricula to the National Agency.

There is a continuous interaction between all levels and layers of the education system, and in times of reform, this conversation becomes even more active. The National Agency carefully follows the needs of municipalities, schools, teachers, and students as well as the challenges in implementing the core curriculum. It analyzes changes in society and follows scientific developments and actively invites people to discuss and work together for common benefit (Halinen & Holappa, 2013).

Local education authorities, principals, and teachers have learned to trust national authorities, and there is mutual respect among them. Similarly, national authorities trust that all municipalities and schools do their best to achieve goals. Parents and various stakeholder groups are also actively involved in developing education.

Trust, respect, and collaborative ethos are probably the most valuable elements in the Finnish education system. It has taken years to build these qualities, and the process has included profound learning, with both successes and mistakes. Next, steps toward systemic and collaborative curriculum reform are examined.

Steps Toward Intensive Interaction, Collaboration, and Trust in Curriculum Reforms

In the process of curriculum reform, there is a long tradition of lively interaction and cooperation. Curriculum development has followed general trends in society, but in education, the desire for continuous conversation and empowerment has been especially strong. The development has taken place through a series of steps over time, as outlined below.

Steps Toward Municipal Curricula in the 1980s

The first step was taken when part of the power in curriculum issues was delegated to municipalities. The 1970 national curriculum for basic education was revised, and the first core curriculum was designed in 1985. Education providers were asked to follow the national process, and, for the first time, obligated to draw up their local curricula based on the national core curriculum.

Steps Toward Power Delegation and School-Based Curricula in 1990s

Since 1985, every new curriculum reform has included even wider and more intensive cooperation. At the beginning of 1990s, the National Agency organized a two-year-long, voluntary experiment that included 12 municipalities and 42 schools that examined ways to produce a school-based curriculum. Schools were called Aquarium schools because everyone interested in them could follow their work and results.

Based on the work of Aquarium schools and municipalities, the core curriculum was revised in 1994. Guidelines at the national level were diminished, and more power was delegated to the local level. All education providers were empowered to draw up their local curriculum and to encourage their schools in designing school-based curricula.

Steps Toward Wide Networks and Intensive Interaction at the Beginning of the 2000s

At the beginning of the 2000s, because of changes in society and the rapid development of technology, it was time to start preparing additional curriculum reform. The National Agency created a wide network of 160 interested municipalities and 315 schools, which were then consulted during the reform process. Local education authorities and schools learned to examine critically the drafts of the core curriculum and give constructive feedback to the National Agency. The new core curriculum was stipulated in 2004, and local curricula were expected to be ready in 2006.

Steps Toward Full Systems Thinking Approach in Curriculum Reform

By 2008, the debate concerning the decline of students' well-being and learning motivation was hectic in Finnish society. At the same time, the quality of learning results was still high in international comparisons, though decreasing a bit. The central questions were: Is schooling still meaningful for students? How could we make learning more enjoyable? How could education better promote sustainable development? These reflections strongly influenced the next round of curriculum reform that started in 2012.

The new core curriculum for basic education was stipulated at the end of 2014, and local curricula were expected to be ready before the start of the autumn term in 2016. This time, it was natural to build the whole reform process on the solid tradition of cooperation. It was even possible to move from cooperation to real dialogue and collaboration, and new digital tools multiplied the opportunities for collective progress.

All municipalities and schools, as well as universities and various stakeholder groups and organizations, were now involved from the very beginning of the reform process. The goals of the reform were carefully discussed, prepared, and published before the actual design process of curriculum documents started. The design process was planned in detail and made as transparent, collaborative, and sustainable as possible. The central idea was to energize municipalities and schools and encourage their innovativeness and understanding of changes in our common world.

THE 2012–2016 CURRICULUM REFORM: AN EXAMPLE OF SYSTEMS THINKING

In Systems Thinking, the central principle is interconnectedness, which refers to how a system's constituent parts interrelate and how the system works within the context of larger systems and over time. In Finland, this interconnectedness is visible, especially in the curriculum, which is a central part of the education system. Changes in society and in the educational system are considered in curriculum development, and accordingly, changes in curriculum promote the development of all other elements of the education system as well as the whole of society.

Besides taking various connections and interrelationships into account, the temporal continuum is also important. Curriculum reform during 2012–2016 was strongly based on the best traditions of the education system and, particularly, respected teachers' experiences and expertise. At the same time, it opened the way to the future. According to Snyder (2023), systems thinking could be defined as a holistic approach that utilizes the analysis of the interrelationships and interdependencies of everything around a common purpose.

This approach challenged people responsible for the reform to deeply reflect on the purpose of the reform. It was understood that without a clear and common purpose, the reform does not make sense to people, and their engagement in the reform remains weak. Interrelationships and interdependencies within the frame of curriculum, as well as between curriculum and other elements around it, were carefully analyzed. Network thinking guided the work at the national level, and local education authorities and schools were encouraged to use the power of teams and networks for designing local curricula.

Many researchers emphasize the importance of feedback as an essential component of systems thinking. Fullan (2010) talks about the collective or collaborative capacity that is needed "to generate the emotional commitment and the technical expertise that no amount of individual capacity working alone can come close to matching" (p. xiii). It really was vital, in the reform, to organize feedback loops and to present clearly how feedback had been influenced. This improved the quality of the documents and promoted the commitment of people who had participated in the reform process with their comments.

Central principles of systems thinking were important guidelines when the curriculum reform process was prepared, organized, and led. Listening to people's opinions, clarifying the purpose of the reform, organizing networks, collaboration, and collective work in order to produce curriculum documents, and creating effective feedback systems were central tasks of the National Agency. To describe the process more concretely, I next examine three important periods of the reform process: the preparatory period, design period, and evaluation period.

Preparatory Period of the Reform Process—Respecting the Past, Orienting to the Future

For the National Agency, careful preparation of the reform was necessary so that all important viewpoints could be considered and a strong knowledge base created for the work. From the viewpoint of the whole nation and education system, it was important to understand where we come from, where we are now, and especially, where do we want to go. Building a solid insight into the direction of development was like drawing a good road map for the reform process. It also helped anticipate expectations, obstacles, and opportunities concerning the change in education.

The period started right after the previous curriculum reform of 2004 by analyzing local and school-based curricula documents, and by collecting information from municipalities and schools: how they had experienced the reform, how they thought they had succeeded in the reform, and what challenges they had encountered.

The National Agency also utilized evaluation documents, produced by the Finnish Education Evaluation Centre, as well as results of various national development projects. These projects deepened and improved certain curricular areas, such as special education, the influence of digitalization, and gender equality. In all projects, networks of municipalities and schools were invited to collaborate, reflect on their experiences, and learn from each other. The National Agency provided prerequisites and guidance for this collective work and then published the results.

A great amount of research information was gathered and analyzed. Various researchers and experts were heard in full-day meetings. Experiences of other well-performing countries and reports of OECD, UNESCO, and the EU were scrutinized as well.

The National Agency also organized meetings and conferences with provincial education authorities, teacher training faculties of universities, textbook publishers, teacher national unions, parent organizations, and municipalities and schools to promote open dialogue and actively listen to thoughts and ideas concerning the renewal of basic education. Students were interviewed in a very large survey—60,000 students answered the survey—and their experiences and wishes were heard in the meetings of the Student Forum.

Simultaneously, the first Future of Learning 2030 Barometer was launched in 2009 by the National Agency (Airaksinen et al., 2017). This new tool was to strengthen the future orientation of the curriculum reform and look beyond contemporary interests. The aim was to acknowledge the alternative futures of education and to take into consideration the possibilities and challenges that may affect the development of schools, teaching, and learning.

The Barometer collected a diversity of arguments on the future. The Delphi method was used as a structured communication technique that took advantage of new technologies and elements of social media. The aim was not a consensus but rather a multivoice view. The Barometer exemplified perfectly the idea of collective capacity, and from this, plans for the actual design period of the core curricula were composed. The design period of the new core curricula officially started at the end of June 2012, when the new Government Decree had been stipulated.

Design Period—Human Networking and Collective Energy in Use

The design period included processes at three levels of the education system: national, municipal, and school. During this period, intensive interaction and mutual learning processes between all these levels were crucial. It generated prerequisites for common problem-solving and the shared creation of curricula.

The design phase at the national level from 2012 to 2014 included the work of officials of the National Agency and the functioning of the Advisory Group, representing central stakeholders, that was nominated for the reform process. The work of all curriculum groups was essential: three generic groups and around 30 specific groups that produced drafts for the new core curricula. Teachers, other school staff, teacher educators, researchers, and local education authorities were represented in these groups, chaired by officials of the National Agency.

Curriculum drafts were published on the National Agency's curriculum website, which was open and accessible to all. Feedback was requested, and a specific tool was created in order to make giving feedback easy. The process was iterative: The received comments influenced the drafts, which were then improved and published again. Municipalities and schools were encouraged to follow the national process, give feedback and, simultaneously, start preparations for their own curriculum work.

During this phase, core curriculum documents and support materials for the local curriculum process were drawn up. Various meetings and training days were organized. The whole process was coordinated, and continuous interaction between the groups was organized by a small coordination group, chaired by the Head of Curriculum Development.

The second design phase included creative design processes of the local curricula. Education providers were empowered to decide how to organize local processes: For instance, should there be only one municipal curriculum or a combination of municipal and school-based curricula? What kind of working groups were formed? How was the collaboration of groups arranged, and how could all teachers, students, parents, and other important stakeholders be involved? The National Agency recommended education providers collaborate with each other and use a participatory approach.

Education providers were urged to collect feedback from their schools concerning the drafts of core curricula and send feedback to the National Agency. In this transparent process, anyone could also give feedback on an open, well-structured website where the drafts were published. During the process, the National Agency produced summaries of the feedback and reported how feedback had influenced the drafts.

The inception of the third phase of the design period was in the autumn term of 2016, when municipalities and schools started working according to the new curricula. Schools in Finland are responsible for creating and carrying out the execution of the new curriculum (Vahtivuori-Hänninen et al., 2014). This implied real changes in teaching and learning processes, other school activities, and in the whole school culture. These changes required school principals and teachers to rethink their work and collaboratively plan school activities, also involving students in planning. The engagement of all school staff was important. Later, some examples of these changes are described.

To improve the quality of the process during these three phases, intensive dialogue and cooperation between the three levels of actors was organized by the National Agency, which created a particular curriculum website and published a planning tool called the Curriculum Roadmap for local actors. Using both of these tools, all essential information concerning the goals and the process of the reform, as well as all core curriculum drafts, were published and easy to reach for anyone. Information was sent to all education providers by the National Agency.

The Curriculum Roadmap described the possible steps that municipalities and schools could take and the topics they could discuss when preparing for local processes. Publishing the drafts during the national design process helped people to comprehend the main goals, principles, and guidelines of the reform as well as to implement them. With each new draft, people could express opinions about the strengths and weaknesses of the reform. All in-service training organized by the National Agency was meant to support local curriculum processes and the final implementation of the new curricula.

Period of Follow-Up, Evaluation, and Research: Quality Control

From the very beginning, research and evaluation were connected with the curriculum reform process in order to analyze and improve its quality. These follow-up activities were allocated by the Ministry of Education and Culture to various actors who worked autonomously. The ministry financed a long-term research project executed by three Finnish universities that focused first on the curriculum design process in the National Agency and later examined local processes and the effects of the new core curriculum on the work of municipalities and schools (Pietarinen et al., 2017).

The Finnish Education Evaluation Centre FINEEC was given the responsibility for a large-scale evaluation of the implementation of the national core curricula for preprimary and basic education in 2014. Evaluations were carried out from 2016 to 2021. The National Agency also conducted surveys and analyses like those made after the 2004 core curriculum reform (see page x, *Preparatory period of the reform process*).

The results of these research and evaluation reports indicate that the actual design process of the core curricula was truly systemic, collaborative, and transparent. The process helped people to make sense of the reform, which then improved their working motivation and commitment to the goals of the reform. During the reform process, information reached municipalities as well, which strengthened the transparency of the process.

However, there were differences between municipalities in how the design processes for local curricula were organized and resourced, especially in how teachers were supported in getting familiar with the goals and guidelines of the reform. For local curriculum processes, better and more frequent state-level support and guidance would have been necessary. But overall, the goals of the reform have been mostly reached, and real changes have been actualized in everyday schoolwork.

New Curriculum Elements Promoting Systems Thinking in Teaching and Learning

The National Core Curriculum for Basic Education 2014 aimed at promoting coherence, interconnectedness, and collaboration in teaching and learning, as well as supporting growth toward a sustainable way of living (Halinen, 2016). New elements, such as transversal competencies and multidisciplinary learning modules, were brought into the curriculum, helping teachers and students to reflect on what is important to teach and study, and why.

Even more important was the question "how?" How are we working, and what do we learn by working in the way we choose? How are various topics connected to each other? Essential skills for sustainable, ethical, and courageous living are developed in the working processes and daily life of schools. The new Core Curriculum included descriptions concerning pervasive knowledge, skills, values, and attitudes that are most needed in the 21st century, as well as the ability to use them in different contexts. These are called transversal competencies.

Seven transversal competencies are: 1) Thinking and learning to learn, 2) Cultural competence, interaction, and self-expression, 3) Taking care of oneself, managing daily life, 4) Multiliteracy, 5) Digital competence, 6) Working-life competence and entrepreneurship, and 7) Participation, involvement, and building a sustainable future.

These competence areas are frequently interconnected and can be promoted in all school subjects and in other activities of the school. The core curriculum emphasizes that the joint objective is to take the students' ages into account, to support growth as human beings, and to impart competencies required for membership in a democratic society and a sustainable lifestyle. It is vital to encourage students to recognize their own uniqueness, personal strengths, and development potential, and to appreciate themselves.

Another new element in the core curriculum, called multidisciplinary learning modules, was meant to be a tool for integrative instruction. The purpose was to enable students to see the relationships and interdependencies among school subjects and the phenomena to be studied. Students are supported to link knowledge and skills of various fields, to understand their connections to the surrounding world, and, in interactive processes with others, to structure them as meaningful entities. The manner and duration of modules may vary depending on the students' needs and the objectives of instruction.

Every student has a right to participate in at least one multidisciplinary learning module every school year. However, teachers and students are planning the modules together so that the studied phenomena are meaningful for students, connect studies with the environment, and ensure the study process is energetic. Learning modules are excellent for developing transversal competencies and for the collaboration of students in multigrade groups and various learning environments. They also promote teachers' mutual collaboration and cooperation with experts outside the school.

The other two central elements in promoting systems thinking and the holistic development of students are school culture and assessment. School culture always affects the quality of schoolwork experienced by students. For the first time, the core curriculum defined principles according to which school culture should be developed. The goal is to create an encouraging culture that makes space for individual and collective reflection and creation; promotes learning, participation, and collaboration; improves well-being; and strengthens a sustainable way of living. They are also guidelines for good leadership.

The role of student assessment in Finland differs from that in most other countries. Emphasis is on formative assessment with which teachers guide and encourage learning and help students to overcome problems in learning. Teachers are expected to give feedback that makes the learning process visible and helps students to perceive and understand a) what they are expected to learn, b) what they have already learned, and c) how they can promote their own learning and improve their performance. Students learn to plan and evaluate their learning process and results and also how to give constructive feedback to their fellow students.

EDUCATION AND CURRICULUM AS ECOSYSTEMS

All elements of the Finnish education system form an ecosystem in which different components work in mutual interaction and support each other (Niemi, 2014). Schools are seen as living and learning organizations that form a part of the broader system.

Respectively, curriculum is understood as an extensive ecosystem in which different areas are linked to each other and together help support the formation of a rich teaching-learning environment with various dimensions (Vahtivuori-Hänninen et al., 2014). The emphasis of the Finnish curriculum is on the mission of guiding holistic educational thinking of schools and municipalities to promote the best possible learning and well-being of students. It allows much space for teachers and students to construct teaching-learning processes and learning environments for their own needs.

Curriculum reforms play an important role in developing the Finnish education system, but as Fullan and Miles (1992) have indicated, reforming the curriculum does not automatically produce sustainable changes in the everyday practices of schools. Fullan (2007) also emphasized that the reform implementation strategy contributes to the reform outcomes.

Pietarinen, Pyhältö and Soini (2017) and their research group have thoroughly analyzed the latest curriculum reform process in Finland. They argued that due to the complex systemic nature of schooling, the reform implementation is simultaneously affected by several complementary, sometimes even contradictory, factors at different levels of education (see also Tikkanen et al., 2017).

According to these researchers, officials responsible for the reform in the National Agency perceived the reform as a systemic entity, comprising several levels of the education system, and affected by multiple factors simultaneously. The officials emphasized, in particular, orchestrating collaboration as a central resource for promoting the reform. Soini et al. (2021) say that this finding implies that the officials considered creating arenas for collective sense-making and promoting stakeholders' participation as a key for reform success. They seemed to recognize well the reform regulators that are in line with the sustainable reform determinants identified in the school reform literature.

According to Pietarinen et al. (2017), the strategy of the reform was identified to represent a combined top-down, bottom-up approach. The top-down, bottom-up approach can be seen in the activities of the National Agency when it utilized the state-level capacity to provide a framework, direction, and resources. It also brought people together and organized networks to create interaction and collaboration that supported reaching goals and promoted curriculum coherence. In the process, the capacity of local-level actors and other stakeholder groups to give critical feedback, create ideas, and find the best solutions were utilized as well.

Researchers indicated that the reform strategy included two distinctive strategic elements: 1) a participative element of extensive knowledge sharing that increased transparency, and 2) a strong steering element of change management (Soini et al., 2021). Transparency and the strong steering element of change management were, in people's minds, associated with successful reform in terms of the perceived educational impact of the reform and curriculum coherence. The reform process exemplified a dialogic mindset and successful use of complexity in pursuit of educational quality.

A CALL TO ACTION

A Systems Thinking approach to educational reforms is possible and, according to the experience of Finland, it is also sustainable. The approach helps us understand that there are no quick or perfect solutions. It is necessary to accept uncertainty and hesitation in front of various conflicting viewpoints and demands and be open to continuous learning and renewal.

Systems thinking guides us to thoroughly prepare long-term reform processes, listen carefully to what people say, and accept contradictory opinions. It is useful in indicating the interrelationships, unexpected connections, and mutual dependencies among the various elements of the system as well as connections outside the system. It emphasizes a continuum: learning from the past and looking to the future.

It is difficult, if not impossible, to find good and sustainable solutions without open dialogue and collective work. Our experience in Finland indicates that it takes time, patience, and determination to build the ethos of trust among the members of the system. To be successful, it is necessary to move toward open, transparent, and collaborative working strategies. Simultaneously, systems thinking addresses the importance of skillful change management as well as passionate and insightful leadership.

Peter Senge says in his foreword for Fullan's book *All Systems Go* (2010): *No institution has a more crucial role to play in the historic changes to come than school because no institution has greater potential to impact how society changes over the long term. How we educate our children shapes the future.* This is the perspective we need. It encourages us to rethink our work in education, and in particular, leadership.

REFERENCES

Airaksinen, T., Halinen, I., & Linturi, H. (2017). Futuribles of learning 2030: Delphi supports the reform of the core curricula in Finland. *European Journal of Futures Research*, 5.

Fullan, M. (2010). *All systems go. The change imperative for whole system reform.* Corwin and Ontario Principal's Council.

Fullan, M., & Miles, M. B. (1992). Getting reform right: What works and what doesn't. *Phi Delta Kappan*, Vol. 73, 745–752.

Halinen, I. (2016). The conceptualization of competencies related to sustainable development and sustainable lifestyles. In *Progress Reflection No. 8 on Current and Critical Issues in Curriculum, Learning and Assessment.* IBE-UNESCO, International Bureau of Education.

Halinen, I., & Holappa, A-S. (2013). Curricular balance based on dialogue, cooperation and trust—the case of Finland. In W. Kuiper & J. Berkvens (Eds.), *Balancing Curriculum Regulation and Freedom across Europe.* CIDREE Yearbook (pp. 39–62).

Halinen, I., Niemi, H., & Toom, A. (2016). La confiance, pierre angulaire du système éducatif en Finlande. *Revue Internationale d'Education de Sevres* (pp. 147–157).

National Core Curriculum for Basic Education 2014. Finnish National Board of Education. Publications 2016:5.

Niemi, H. (2014). The Finnish educational ecosystem. In Niemi et al. (Eds.), *Finnish Innovations and Technologies in Schools* (pp. 3–19). Rotterdam: Sense Publishers.

Niemi, H., Toom, A., & Kallioniemi, A. (2012). *Miracle of education: The principles and practices of teaching and learning in Finnish schools*. Rotterdam: Sense Publishers.

Pietarinen, J., Pyhältö, K., & Soini, T. (2017). Large-scale curriculum reform in Finland—exploring the interrelation between implementation strategy, the function of the reform, and curriculum coherence. *The Curriculum Journal*, 28(1), 22–40.

Tikkanen, L., Pyhältö, K., Soini, T., & Pietarinen J. (2017). Primary determinants of a large-scale curriculum reform—National board administrators' perspectives. *Journal of Educational Administration*, 55(6), 702–716.

Snyder, K. J. (2023). Systems thinking and sustainable schooling: Foundations in physics. In K. J. Snyder & K. M. Snyder (Eds.), *Systems Thinking for Sustainable Schooling: A Mindshift for Education to Lead and Achieve Quality in Schools*. Rowman & Littlefield.

Soini, T., Pyhältö, K., & Pietarinen, J. (2021). Shared sense-making as key for large scale curriculum reform in Finland. In M. Priestley, D. Alvunger, S. Philippou, & T. Soini (Eds.), *Curriculum making in Europe: Policy and practice within and across diverse contexts* (pp. 247–272). Emerald Publishing Limited.

Vahtivuori-Hänninen, S., Halinen, I., Niemi, H., Lavonen, J., & Lipponen, L. (2014). A new Finnish national core curriculum for basic education and technology as an integrated tool for learning. In Niemi et al. (Eds.), *Finnish Innovations and Technologies in Schools* (pp. 21–32). Rotterdam: Sense Publishers.

Chapter 2

Leadership Preparation for Sustainable Schooling

Michele Acker-Hocevar

There is growing pressure to transform static university educational leadership preparation programs into more dynamic, relevant, and experiential models that better prepare educational leaders for the exigencies they face today and into the future. This chapter argues that meeting the challenges of the changing world is only possible through a framework of sustainable schooling, systems thinking and new mindsets that can guide reform. The canary in the coal mine has sung. The tipping point for survival depends on if the call is heeded.

Evidence from teachers, administrators, students, community members, and professors regarding their overall dissatisfaction with the current educational system has been voiced. School personnel resignations, the common view that education is increasingly irrelevant for future employment, and public outcries from parents over school policies and various curricula are all concerning for institutional viability. On one level, these trends suggest a much deeper, national systemic problem with many of our institutions. On another level, there is a national awakening that will take a different mindset to prepare educational leaders for the future.

The purpose of this chapter is to explore a different approach to leadership preparation drawing upon the writings of Halinen (2017), who describes eight lessons learned from the development and implementation of the National Core Curriculum of 2014 in Finland. I will use these eight lessons in my discussion and recommendations about how to reform leadership preparation programs today. It is critical for this call to be heard. Educational leaders have the knowledge, experiences, and tools to shape changes that must be made instead of continuing to justify unsustainable practices.

This chapter is divided into two parts. Part I addresses the current context surrounding leadership preparation and argues for why the eight lessons can aid us in the unwieldy discussion about reform of educational leadership preparation programs. Part II applies the lessons to current leadership preparation programs to explore how they can be reimagined. The analysis is guided by a tripod lens based on formative, educative, and transformative questions.

The formative reflects the "what" of leadership preparation, the educative examines the "how" to support leadership preparation, and the transformative explores "why" it is important to reform educational leadership. I recognize that these lessons reflect the Finnish experience. Nonetheless, they are foundational to understanding deep reform and change in ways to initiate a process in the United States. Implications from the lessons are woven together in a Call to Action, with suggestions for how to begin the process.

By viewing leadership preparation through this tripod lens of formative, educative and transformative, the journey can begin. Legacies of mass production that ignore contextual variety are obsolete. Divisions of labor, or the assembly-line model of moving from course to course, can be replaced with an integrated systems model that recognizes different levels of preparation. Bureaucratic mindsets, too slow to adapt to environmental changes, can now become a responsive network organization connecting others to ideas that promote organizational agility and responsiveness through quantum power relationships to adapt to environmental changes

LEADERSHIP TODAY AND THE NEED FOR A MIND SHIFT

Leadership today has been described as a landscape comprised of "increasing levels of Volatility, Uncertainty, Complexity, and Ambiguity (VUCA)" (Lilja et al., 2022, p. 1). This does not mean that leaders should feel they are steering a rudderless ship on a stormy sea. Rather, it means leaders need more sophisticated navigational tools at their disposal that can guide their journeys to focus their energies on desired destinations.

Leaders must have mental models that shape, prioritize, and allocate resources with new ways of thinking about how to anchor their decision-making in systems thinking for continual improvement around shared beliefs, values, and practices. This is a process of decision-making that promotes sustainability and prepares students for the future at the forefront of every leader's mind. Fortunately, if leaders develop a robust and shared culture that links people, programs, services, and practices around a shared vision, purposive and meaningful actions will ensue. The system will continuously evolve, adapt, and self-renew.

Dead ends, which are barriers and obstacles that thwart optimal leadership actions, will be less likely to occur. Motivation, internalized because of trusting the process, frees everyone to engage in meaningful work. The result is harmony and unity of working together with the potential for creativity and attending to what arises naturally and sustainably.

In other words, too many leadership programs educate future leaders with obsolete mindsets that ensure failure (Cunningham et al., 2019). Working in isolation instead of knowing how to develop collaborative and team-based structures and top-down communicative processes will stoke resentment and set people up for failure. It is professional negligence to have people working in isolation; it is inherently unsustainable.

Positive connections sustain and generate innovations, which often lead to breakthroughs that can be shared within a learning culture. Leaders of today must recognize that their role is to engage others, not to control them. Because there are so many revolutions occurring in the wider scientific and technological spheres to be considered, a leader can't know everything and be everything. Therefore, rethinking leadership preparation curricula means leaders must know how to better identify individual talents, design sustainable systems, and build on systems strengths.

The ability to assemble and develop teams capable of continuous improvement, adaptation, and learning is paramount. Essentially, the leader's understanding of new ways of thinking matters in how they communicate, educate, manage change, and design network organizational structures (Snyder & Snyder, 2021). A revolutionary mind shift needs to occur at all levels to apply learning instead of only acquiring it. New insights gained from others through such things as nationally recognized exemplary programs and the ground-breaking work of authors such as Snyder and Snyder (2021) on systems thinking must guide leadership preparation work.

This chapter is not about incremental change but radically overhauling delivery platforms, revamping curricular frameworks, and forging more trusting relationships. The outcome is to have a positive energy system that involves all educational players. These overdue reforms beg for ethically sound, mentally healthy, and mature individuals to promote collaborative learning over self-interest among and across practitioners, mentors, professors, community members, and policymakers.

Leaders who embrace an interdisciplinary understanding bring coherence and relevance to leadership preparation programs. These leaders connect with other like-minded people and focus on the changes to be made. This requires a different fund of knowledge for reflection, listening, engaging in messy problems, and honing verbal and written communication skills. These are activist leaders who see conflict as an opportunity to develop learning around the strengths of self and others while challenging underlying beliefs rooted in fear of change.

Reconsidering Leadership Preparation Based on the Eight Lessons

In Halinen's (2017) report about the Finnish educational system, she writes:

> Upper secondary education is comprised of either general (that is, academic) or vocational education. Both forms of education are equally popular among young people, and they provide eligibility for tertiary education. There are no dead ends in the Finnish education system. Rather, all students are supported in their studies so they can go as far as possible toward fulfilling their potential. (p. 7)

This noble idea of no dead ends in the Finnish education system inspired my critical thinking about what, how, and why radical reform has been so slow in the United States. Just as niche marketing is accepted practice today, a one-size-all approach to leadership preparation and schooling, in general, does not fit with the current environment. How are educational leaders to prepare students for the future if the rhetoric of reform maintains the status quo? To meet the challenges of the future, leadership preparation programs must break free from the organizational quagmire of archaic roles and institutional expectations that are unsustainable.

Understanding how to manage the change process that forms the VUCA landscape can be traveled with hope and collaboration if the proper understandings are there. Yes, there are storm warnings ahead on the horizon, but leaders, at all levels, must pay heed to the call for reform and know how best to navigate these storms through fresh learning and new mindsets. Again, the storm warnings and the canary singing in the coal mine call forth the need for change.

When leaders ground their knowledge in modelling what is needed, they can educate others on their journeys. It is not about having all the answers. It is about understanding how to manage a change process. The group can learn, and skills can be developed. The leaders facilitate the process with tools in place to constantly gather input they feed into the system to make course corrections.

The eight lessons from Halinen (2017, 33–35). are:

1. Know your history and build on your strengths.

2. Utilize the best experiences from other countries, as well as findings from research, evaluations, and development projects of your own country. Build a strong knowledge base for the reform.
3. Take care of sustainability in the curriculum-planning process: empower individuals and communities and look for community-based solutions.
4. Look at the complex world around school and focus on shared visions, values, and faith in the future.
5. Analyze and include all dimensions of sustainability in the curriculum: decide on the concepts you want to use and explain their meaning.
6. Notice that competencies needed in the complex world include knowledge, skills, values, attitudes, and resolve.
7. Focus on understanding the big picture and learning by experience.
8. Focus on students' all-around development and sustainable well-being (sustainable well-being refers to pursuing a good life within the Earth's carrying capacity).

Lesson One: Know Your History and Build on Strengths

This first lesson asks educational leaders to know their history. From a formative aspect, there are several books written about the U.S. educational system and what conclusions might be drawn from it. For example, in the book *Education and the Cult of Efficiency*, Callahan (1964) portrays how educators sought legitimacy with prevailing organizational forms by adopting a corporate model for organizational arrangements.

From this formative perspective, or the "what" of leadership preparation, there are many examples of how early decisions resulted in a culture of conformity, resulting in leadership preparation courses that were very similar across the United States. The more prominent institutions had more leeway to break away from the status quo. However, within the history of education, there has been pressure to reform educational practices. National goals turned into national standards, followed by state standards and national standardized yearly tests. Leadership accountability became testing accountability.

These bureaucratic mechanisms to control and tighten what is taught impacted educational leadership programs to align leadership preparation more closely to raising standardized test results. Underlying systemic problems of student achievement ignored contextual differences. Educators responded by saying, "You cannot mandate what matters."

The "what" of educational leadership preparation suggests similar course listings across traditional programs, although, their delivery and content may vary significantly. From my experience, leadership preparation courses generally yielded little learning. Furthermore, the course content "covered" lagged significantly behind present-day understandings of the actual field. It was not unusual to see a leadership book in its 7th or 8th edition, with only minor updates, used in many educational leadership preparation programs. Again, this is a legacy of conformity, not innovation.

For example, I typed in "principal certification program" in my search engine, resulting in a page from Point Park University Principal Certificate Program. On this site, a fully online K–12 school principal certification program is 18-credit graduate hours. The online program is asynchronous. Courses are Educational Administration, the Principalship, Clinical Supervision and Leadership, Applied Research Practicum I: School Administrator-School Principal K–12, Applied Research Practicum II: School Administrator-School Principal K–12, and Differentiated Instructional Practices. A master's degree is required in education (student's choice) along with the courses mentioned earlier.

A description of one of the courses follows:

> EDUC 538 Educational Administration (3). This course provides the supervisor in training with a foundation of the educational theories and research that affect the day-to-day administration of schools. Topics will include theories of organization, educational foundations, and structures, supervision of personnel, collaboration and team-building, interdisciplinary curriculum design, effective job analysis procedures, staff performance appraisals, and technology issues. This course is designed to examine and analyze the means for managing institutional resources in educational settings, with an emphasis on human, fiscal, and physical resources. There is a focus on Pennsylvania school budgeting procedures as the course considers the development of practical skills in resource management in school finance and school plant operations.

In contrast, at the University of Chicago (using the search "leadership preparation"), an online certification in Conscious Leadership and Team Management appeared from their College of Business and Management. A brief description follows because it is in sharp contrast to the description from Point Park University:

> The University of Chicago's professional development certificate in Conscious Leadership and Team Management equips professionals with the tools and skills needed to advance into leadership positions. The certificate offers training in self-assessment and management theory, with students building a foundation of professional excellence to manage teams and individuals with confidence. The online program with synchronous sessions employs a multi-pronged approach to creative leadership, the handling of complex problems, and navigating change.

The description continues:

Extraordinary leaders are thoughtful and intentional, able to pull from the myriad solutions in their toolbox to manage organizations and human capital. For each apparent obstacle, leaders must remain open and honest, recognizing that success and failure begin and end with their ability to be self-aware, socially competent, and appreciative of relationships at each level of the business.

From an educative perspective, or "how" to support the leadership of self and others, the description from Point Park focuses on how to manage buildings, finances, and personnel. The historical remnants of the superintendent as an overseer of buildings, buses, and finances appear. Although necessary for someone to take charge, this relic from the past is hardly sufficient to prepare leaders today or relevant to the role of a leader today in developing people (Darling-Hammond et al., 2010).

In contrast, the University of Chicago's approach to conscious leadership and team development appears more in line with contemporary school and organizational development based on the VUCA model and systems theory (Lilja et al., 2022; Snyder et al., 2008). From an educative perspective, the history of education can shed light on why certain innovations were never implemented. Exploring these contemporary needs may be useful.

The transformative, or "why" certain courses and experiences are important in a digital and network world, becomes critical to building a unifying framework, grounded in systems thinking and quality management. Standards for quality leadership like the Baldrige Leadership Award, noticeably absent from these examples, appear absent in many programs and school reform models (Snyder, 2023). Snyder and Björkman (2016) posit that contemporary school leadership is strengthened significantly by a systems view of leading schools.

Knowing history so as not to repeat the failed reforms of the past is important. Designing a coherent program for educational leaders should connect history to the present to identify why and how certain strengths from history can help shape the future change process.

Lesson Two: Utilize the Best Experiences from Other Countries: Build a Strong Knowledge Base for the Reform

This lesson asks those who design leadership preparation programs to learn from others. From a formative perspective, or the "what" of leadership preparation, the University Council for Educational Administration (UCEA) is one example of an organization dedicated to professors of educational leadership to promote excellence in the preparation of educational leaders. As such, one of the organization's publications, the *Journal of Research on Leadership Education* (JRLE), publishes articles on leadership preparation.

As a past coeditor of JRLE when UCEA initiated its award program(s) of excellence, I selected two programs in 2013 for their excellence: the University of Illinois-Chicago's EdD, Urban Education Leadership, and the University of Texan-San Antonio's, Urban School Leaders Collaborative. Both these award winners were sensitive to contextual needs in the design of their programs, and both programs incorporated leadership standards into program design and incorporated a means for continuous evaluation.

Significantly, since the inception of the award, only four awards have been given in the nine years. For three years, two programs received awards. And in one year, only one program award was given. After nine years, a total of seven programs of excellence were awarded. Both North Carolina and Washington received two awards for different leadership preparation programs, which is a little over 50 percent of all the awards given.

From an educative perspective, or how to support the leadership of self and others, there are some "how[s]" for those reforming leadership preparation to consider across these award institutions. First, the professors at these award-winning universities provided strong evidence in their documentation about how they continuously assessed their programs' efficacy to make ongoing improvements. Second, the program faculty had strong connections with the practitioners in their areas and had trusting relationships with them.

Third, the professors worked collaboratively with each other as well as with members in the field. Fourth, courses were often cotaught with a practitioner. Fifth and most importantly, students practiced their learning in authentic settings within a culture of rich feedback. Sixth, there was a culture of continuous improvement that required an "all-hands-on-deck" attitude. Finally, these award-winning programs had university professors willing to find institutional and other financial support to sustain their innovative programs.

The transformative, or why these programs broke away from the traditional and conformist models of preparing school leaders, may best be understood in their listening to what was needed in the field and their willingness to engage in reform efforts at their institutions. Cosner (2019) describes how collaboration was at the center of the work done at the University of Illinois-Chicago's EdD, Urban Education Leadership program.

Professors at the University of Washington collected feedback and listened to what school leaders had to say about their preparation experiences, and they fed improvements into the system to adjust (Cosner, 2019). Each of these award-winning programs designed a sustainable model of improvement through listening, collaboration, and a partnership orientation within their respective contexts.

Lesson Three: Take Care of Sustainability in the Curriculum-Planning Process: Empower Individuals and Communities and Look for Community-Based Solutions

From a formative perspective, or the "what" of leadership preparation, sustainability in the curriculum begins with creating the space for those reforming the programs to work and be recognized for that work. Cosner (2019) states that present university tenure requirements work against this type of collaborative work needed for reform.

Often, and particularly in large school districts in the United States, a parallel process to socialize and prepare school leaders is embedded in job-related training within the school district. This works in very large urban school districts but is difficult in smaller and more rural school districts where networks form the basis for ongoing training and support.

Professors will often forge partnerships outside the traditional university boundaries to work directly with school districts. This was the case with Snyder and Andersen when they worked with the top leadership in Pasco County, Florida, to implement Managing Productive Schools. There, a systems view of professional development created a unique community with a shared language for ongoing leadership and school development (Snyder et al., 2008).

From an educative perspective, or "how" to support the leadership of self and others, there must be tiered levels of support (Sedlack & Scanga, 2023). There are some examples of how universities have worked with their school districts to begin this process (Cosner et al., 2018; Reyes-Guerra et al., 2014). The early certification process of educational leaders should be the initial step in the school leader's preparation that lays a knowledge foundation, coupled with experiential learning.

Systems thinking, quality management, continuous improvement, and assessment are critical for leaders to develop and lead and sustain schools today. Internal work structures based on teams, networking, and partnerships are also vital. As well, establishing trusting community relationships, identifying outside connections for life-long learning, and ongoing professional development are the bedrock of this foundational learning for preparing principals with the skills and knowledge for what is needed to lead schools today (Snyder & Snyder, 2021).

From a transformative perspective, or the "why," leadership preparation programs should consider a tiered perspective with different aspirations for each tier to ensure that there is the sustainability of leaders within their roles. Without robust connections with colleagues and the time to reflect, question, learn, and act, leadership can become a lonely endeavor. If the foundation is on solid ground, then extended opportunities to learn and grow will add to an ongoing and dynamic process.

Lesson 4: Take a Look at the Complex World around School and Focus on Shared Visions, Values, and Faith in the Future

From a formative perspective, the "what" of leadership preparation programs must be aware that the fourth industrial revolution will be unlike anything seen in the prior three industrial revolutions. Knowing the history of these changes will put into perspective how quickly changes are occurring in the present. It will also help to identify gaps in current practice (Crow & Whiteman, 2016).

From an educative perspective, or the "how" to develop self and others, there are connections through networks to inform the leader and others about significant future changes. If you ask young adults if they think their high school education prepared them for the future, most of them will laugh. Even my preteen grandson, knowing my educational background and not wanting to offend me, said that schools could do more to help students apply their learning.

From a transformative perspective, or the "why" of having values and faith in the future, designers of preparation programs must provide prospective leaders with a fund of knowledge about how to embrace the unknown through valuing collaboration with others. Working in networks and staying abreast of future trends is also critical. Leaders need not be fearful but rather empowered with the skills and capacities to be innovative and create learning spaces that are in line with the values needed to support a sustainable future.

Lesson Five: Analyze and Include All Dimensions of Sustainability in the Curriculum: Decide on the Concepts You Want to Use and Explain Their Meaning

From a formative perspective of "what," sustainability must serve as the starting place for educators, including a shared understanding of what it means. This can occur in each district through different forums and with educational partners and university professors. This will invariably involve identifying dimensions of the concept that are mutually and reciprocally beneficial and agreed upon for short and long-term benefit and assessment over time.

From an educative perspective, or the "how" to develop self and others, leadership preparation programs can engage in a process of defining what sustainability means and how it will be enacted. Once there is agreement about what it is, there should also be agreement about what is unsustainable.

After a broad-based consensus, dimensions of sustainability benchmarks can assess where the school is regarding its development.

From a transformative perspective, or the "why" of having a shared understanding of sustainability, this understanding, equipped with data gathered on various dimensions of sustainability, feed back into the school system recommendations from different role groups about how to move forward.

Lesson Six: Notice the Competencies Needed in the Complex World, Including Knowledge, Skills, Values, Attitudes, and Resolve

From a formative perspective, of the "what" of educational leadership preparation, leaders must be knowledgeable in all the areas previously mentioned in this chapter. These include, but are not limited to: systems thinking, change management, quantum thinking, individual and organizational development, network theory, quality management, appreciative inquiry, positive psychology, ongoing assessment, research, and evaluation, and organizational arrangements that promote structures for team learning and collaboration.

From a formative perspective, skills such as listening, reflection, problem-solving, conflict resolution, goal setting, communication skills, strategic thinking, empathy, and trust are important. Values include integrity, trust, empathy, inclusiveness, generosity, cooperativeness, equitable practices, fairness, love, and courage. Attitudes include acceptance, caring, respectfulness, flexibility, hopefulness, optimism, professionalism, and tolerance.

From an educative perspective of "how" to develop self and others, leadership preparation programs should determine how best to assess these various areas and provide supports where needed. Many of these areas can be folded into experiential learning activities within real-life settings where feedback is provided. Self-assessments and general assessments should benchmark a plan of action for the development of self and others.

From a transformative perspective, or the "why" of this lesson in leadership preparation, resolve comes from the strength of knowing oneself and trusting others to come through on difficult tasks. Frequently, leaders fail because they have not taken the time to know who they are and develop strong relationships with others who would have their backs. Being clear about values, attitudes, and levels of skill development is the "why" that leaders need to align their actions with who they are and foster close and authentic relationships.

Lesson Seven: Focus on Understanding the Big Picture and Learning by Experiences

From a formative perspective, of the "what" of leadership preparation, Sullivan (2023) anchors her strategic decision-making within a strategic leadership philosophy that builds on her background as a counselor before becoming a high school principal. She led her school's development and community engagement by paying attention to patterns occurring in her school. She trusted her intuition to see the big picture to guide the collective work of the school's continuous improvement process. This illustrates to Cunningham et al. (2019) that powerful learning experiences need to be included in principal preparation programs.

From the "how" of leadership preparation in supporting self and others, Sullivan understood that helpful organizational arrangements (i.e., teachers, students, parents, and community) allowed educators to work together around a shared and common purpose. She intentionally built these connections into her school.

From the "why" or transformative perspective, creating these structures allowed everyone to contribute and feel valued. Likewise, Halinen (2017) "emphasized that it is important to conduct the curriculum reform process sustainably and, through that, to create the best possible circumstances for high-quality teaching and learning" (p. 33). Halinen grasped, as did Sullivan, that building trusting relationships over time, and creating structures within organizational arrangements were necessary for people to engage with each other and others. Intuitively, it appears that Halinen knew what Sullivan knew. Trust the process. It works.

Lesson Eight: Focus on Students' All-Around Development and Sustainable Well-Being

From a formative perspective, or the "what" of leadership preparation program reform and development, it should be clear by now that program development must consider the whole person in an integrated model that invites ongoing feedback to the learner about their progress. This does not mean everyone needs the same things.

From an educative perspective, or the "how" to develop self and others, students in preparation programs should be given multiple experiences and opportunities to have feedback about themselves and others. This is much more helpful in a safe learning setting than in a school where there is open resentment and hostility because of poor leadership and miscalculations on where people are regarding certain areas.

From a transformative perspective, or the "why" of reforming educational preparation programs, the overall conclusion is that programs must be holistic, offer a healthy way of thriving and optimize living and experiencing—the essence of life. Understanding relationships as inseparable patterns that will evolve as designers of preparation programs dive into the creative energies of nourishing constant emergence should be a driving force of change.

A CALL TO ACTION

Educational leaders are the spokespersons and gatekeepers of the nation's educational institutions. They cannot model a quantum worldview of responsive power (Acker-Hocevar, 2023); put into practice what we know from the quality management organizational literature (Snyder, 2023); incorporate the new sciences as a philosophy for change and adaptive learning (Snyder & Snyder, 2021), build strong networks for connections and sharing ideas (Snyder & Snyder, 2021), and promote innovations that inform naturally the evolution of a living and dynamic system if they don't understand what this means (Snyder, 2023).

There is too much at stake now to ignore the forces at play pushing institutions to evolve naturally through partnerships and connections with others. Capra and Luisi (2016) state that traditionally, new learnings came from quantitative measures, ignoring the complexity of the whole or qualitative measures. Each of us is an expert from our own experiences that inform how we think about school leadership. It is the qualitative things this chapter addresses that are at the heart of reforming school leadership programs. It is about the relationships of the leader to self, and others and the systems approach to connect the dots of reform.

It is about building on strengths, where life can be supported and sustained. Leaders are aware of venerated values sacred to moving to the future. They know that honoring traditions may not mean keeping these traditions. They understand that in a systems understanding, knowledge connects biological, cognitive, social, and ecological dimensions of life (Capra & Luisi, 2016). It is interdisciplinary.

How do you begin the process of reform? Give up an attachment to any particular outcome and look at what we know. Put everything on the table. Frame your reform with a systems view of life. Come up with evident strengths. Build on them. Become a knowledge producer. Engage in collaboration with others. Build partnerships and networks. Consider suggestions in this chapter. Then dive in. There is no recipe, but the program designers must have an integrated conceptual model that builds on strengths and connections.

REFERENCES

Acker-Hocevar, M. (2023). A Quantum worldview of responsive power for sustainable learning. In K. J. Snyder and K. M. Snyder (Eds.), *Systems thinking for sustainable schooling: A mindset for educators to lead and achieve quality schools.* Lanham, MD: Roman & Littlefield Publishers.

Callahan, R. E. (1964). *Education and the cult of efficiency.* University of Chicago Press.

Cosner, S. (2019). What makes a leadership preparation program exemplary? *Journal of Research on Leadership Education*, 14(1), 98–115.

Cosner, S., De Voto, C., & Andry Rah'man, A. (2018). Drawing in the school context as a learning resource in school leader development: Application-oriented projects in active learning designs. *Journal of Research on Leadership Education*, 13(3), 238–255.

Crow, G. M., & Whiteman, R. S. (2016). Effective preparation program features A literature review. *Journal of Research on Leadership Education*, 11(1), 120–148.

Cunningham, K. M., Van Gronigen, B. A., Tucker, P. D., & Young, M. D. (2019). Using powerful learning experiences to prepare school leaders. *Journal of Research on Leadership Education*, 14(1), 74–97.

Darling-Hammond, L., LaPointe, M., Meyerson, D., & Orr, M. (2007). *Preparing school leaders for a changing world: Executive summary.* Stanford, CA: Stanford University, Stanford Educational Leadership Institute.

Halinen, I. (2017). The conceptualization of competencies related to sustainable development and sustainable lifestyles. Paris: UNESCO: *International Bureau of education series, current and critical issues in curriculum, learning and assessment.*

Lilja, J., Snyder, K. M., Sten, & L-M. (2022). Teaming for quality in the VUCA landscape: Exploring key elements for the next progressive leap in team-based practices to drive quality, sustainability, and regeneration. Paper presentation at the 28th Annual Conference, International Sustainable Development Research Society (ISDRS). Stockholm.

Reyes-Guerra, D., Russo, M. R., Bogotch, I. E., & Vásquez-Colina, M. D. (2014). Building a school leadership programme: an American paradox of autonomy and accountability. *School Leadership & Management*, 34(4), 414–437.

Scanga, D., & Sedlack, R. (2023). Networking for principal sustainability. In K. J. Snyder & K. M. Snyder (Eds.), *Systems thinking for sustainable schooling: A mindset for educators to lead and achieve quality schools.* Lanham, MD: Rowman & Littlefield Publishers.

Snyder, K. J. (2023). Systems thinking and sustainable schooling: Foundations in physics. In K. J. Snyder & K. M. Snyder (Eds.), *Systems thinking for sustainable schooling: A mindset for educators to lead and achieve quality schools.* Lanham, MD: Rowman & Littlefield Publishers.

Snyder, K. M. (2023). Expanding how we think about quality in education. In K. J. Snyder & K. M. Snyder (Eds.), *Systems thinking for sustainable schooling: A mindset for educators to lead and achieve quality schools.* Lanham, MD: Rowman & Littlefield Publishers.

Snyder, K. J., & Snyder, K. M. (2021). Building sustainable systems for schooling in turbulent times: Big ideas from the sciences. In Jeffrey Glanz (Ed.), *Crisis and pandemic leadership: Implications for meeting the needs of students, teachers and parents*. Lanham, MD: Rowman and Littlefield Publishers.

Snyder, K. M., & Björkman, C. (2016). Systematisk skol- och kvalitetsutveckling med SWCP school work culture profile. I Metodhandbok för förskolechefer och rektorer. Stockholm: Studentlitteratur AB.

Snyder, K. J., Acker-Hocevar, M., & Snyder, K. M. (2008). *Living on the edge of chaos: Leading schools into the global age*. Milwaukee, WI: ASQ Quality Press.

Sullivan, E. (2023). The quantum school leader as a strategic systems thinker. In K. J. Snyder & K. M. Snyder (Eds.), *Systems thinking for sustainable schooling: A mindset for educators to lead and achieve quality schools*. Lanham, MD: Rowman & Littlefield Publishers.

Chapter 3

Principal Networking for School Sustainability

Renee Sedlack, David Scanga, Tammy Berryhill, and Claudia Steinacker

The school principal is crucial to the success of a school, influencing several important factors: academic achievement, teacher retention, maintaining a positive school culture, community engagement, and partnerships. A looming exodus of school leaders threatens the sustainability of schooling as we know it today. The data we are about to present on principal retention is worrisome; however, keep in mind that disequilibrium in a system creates energy that allows solutions to emerge. One of those solutions can be found in building principal networks. This chapter examines the principalship challenges and tells a success story of one district's effort to network beginning principals that was pivotal to sustaining school leadership.

Today's principals feel an overwhelming responsibility to achieve at the highest level and, at the same time, feel a loss of power and control over decisions needed to improve the learning environment. The combination of aspirations to be a high achiever and loss of autonomy produces undue strain on most leaders, resulting in stress and burnout. According to satisfaction data collected by the RAND Corporation, principals' job satisfaction is at an all-time low (Superville, 2022).

Additional information from a survey by the National Association of Secondary School Principals released in December 2021 revealed that 38 percent of principals planned to leave their jobs within the next three years (NASSP, 2021). Researchers concluded that the loss of school leaders would disproportionally affect historically marginalized communities, students of color, and those from impoverished communities. The Hechinger Report, published by a nonprofit, independent news organization, revealed that as far back as 2015, 30 percent of principals who lead troubled schools left every year (Tyre, 2015).

In terms of those new to the role, research has revealed that one out of every two novice principals are not retained beyond their third year on the job (NASSP, 2017). By year three, more than half of all principals leave their jobs (Tyre, 2015). Let us consider influencing factors.

The problem has been magnified more recently by the population increase in the United States resulting in the need for 6 percent more school leaders in elementary, middle, and high schools (NASSP, 2017). The principal pipeline is also affected by the current teacher shortage in our country (NASSP, 2021). In a study focused on the well-being of principals during the pandemic, researchers found that four out of five secondary school principals experienced frequent job-related stress during the 2020–2021 school year (Woo & Steiner, 2021).

While this is recognized as a national crisis, there is not a widespread organized effort to retain principals. In places like Dallas, Chicago, and Philadelphia, a few newly organized initiatives focus on principal support with on-the-job training, leadership coaching, and hands-on practice in schools (Fabel, 2016). More is undoubtedly needed if we wish to stem the tide of leaders departing from the districts and schools. A systems approach is needed in these turbulent times if we hope to retain school leaders through what has become a major school crisis.

ISSUES AFFECTING PRINCIPAL RETENTION

It is worthwhile to consider how school leadership challenges have become more complex and magnified by the effects of the pandemic on education in the United States. The pandemic accelerated the stress points on school leaders, leading many to question whether to continue in the role. During the 2020–2021 school year, secondary school principals indicated that job stressors included supporting teachers' well-being, students' social-emotional learning, and pandemic-related challenges (Woo & Steiner, 2021). Principals of color, female principals, and those who led high-poverty schools were especially likely to experience job-related stress.

The tense political atmosphere resulting from the impact of the pandemic on schools is a contributing factor to school leaders' decisions to leave the profession (NASSP, 2021). In the NASSP study conducted by an independent research firm with a representative sample of over 500 public, private, and charter school principals, more than one-third of principals reported receiving online and in-person threats in response to the steps they had taken to prevent the spread of COVID-19 in their school. Twenty percent reported that these threats have made them much less likely to continue as principals (Ruggirello, 2022).

In addition to the pandemic in 2020–2021, the nation's schools experienced significant crises such as racial and social justice issues, a divisive election cycle, and a multitude of severe weather events (NAESP, 2021). These situations have contributed to the increase in concerns about the mental health and well-being of both students and staff, as well as the school leaders themselves (McMurdock, 2022). Principals reported that their responsibilities expanded beyond the typical duties to include crisis management and communicating with highly politicalized community groups with conflicting perspectives (NAESP, 2021).

Besides these emerging challenges, principals surveyed reported that heavy workloads and state and local accountability measures were contributing factors to their consideration to leave the profession (Ruggirello, 2022). In the National Association of Secondary School Principals survey, principals indicated that a challenging aspect of their job was implementing the abundance of district and state policies (NASSP, 2021). This is worthy of further discussion.

Perhaps one of the greatest threats to principal retention is the lack of support from district staff. The same survey reported that only one in four principals feel the support they receive meets their needs (NASSP, 2021). In addition, the report from the National Association of Elementary Principals suggests that while the role of the principal has evolved to become more complex, no corresponding support and resources have followed (Ruggirello, 2022).

The researchers (NASSP, 2021) focusing on the well-being of principals one year into the COVID pandemic suggest that support for principals' well-being along with resources to help them manage the operational aspects of their job would be beneficial. Support networks for new and seasoned principals are highly recommended giving opportunities for sharing experiences and collaboration in problem-solving.

The most significant finding is the importance of elevating the voice of the principal early in the decision-making process (Ruggirello, 2022). Seventy-seven percent of secondary school principals would like opportunities to connect with colleagues experiencing the same challenges (NASSP, 2021). It is significant to note that, in this same survey, respondents strongly believed that principal networks would be beneficial to enhance professional knowledge and leadership skills (NAESP, 2021). They are asking to be networked! Providing meaningful coaching and professional development are also worthwhile strategies (NASSP, 2022; Woo & Steiner, 2021).

It is critical that we understand ways to retain talented and effective school leaders responsible for the dynamic change needed in today's schools, both locally and internationally. We must first listen to principals to fully understand the challenges of the current role of leading a school in today's world. To that end, this chapter highlights three current studies, all completed in a single central Florida school district over the span of two years that focus on challenges principals face and a possible solution for the sustainability of quality schooling.

The first two studies emphasize what principals are saying about the difficulties of their jobs and the district support that would help them achieve success. The first study highlights the importance of empowerment and autonomous decision-making at the school level. Principals highly value the ability to adapt and change within the context of each school. Plus, empowerment leads to intrinsic motivation, one reason researchers say people are inclined to stay in their jobs.

The second study focuses on the right kind of district support for principals, especially novice principals, who face unparalleled challenges. Principals shared that the district's pipeline for recruitment was intact, but training was needed to prepare them for the challenges they faced once they were appointed as principals. The one exception to the lack of district support was a network experience that offered them an ongoing opportunity to connect with other principals.

The third study was experiential and shares a network model that addresses the same concerns the principals highlighted in the first two studies. If we are listening to principals, then the third study describes a replicable solution to many of the problems faced by today's school leaders. It is a story about the positive impact networking can have on principals' professional growth and well-being. Networks increase the self-efficacy of principals and increase the likelihood of long-term service.

JOB SATISFACTION, SCHOOL CONTEXT, AND AUTONOMOUS DECISION-MAKING OF SCHOOL PRINCIPALS

As stated in the previous section of this chapter, the recruitment and retention of principals have become hypercritical, with one in five schools losing its principal each year (Henry & Harbatkin, 2019). Determining the antecedents contributing to principal stability in a school will help create sustainability in student achievement and positive school change.

The study, *Factors impacting elementary retention: job satisfaction, school context, and autonomous decision-making*, completed in this central Florida school district, surveyed principals on key drivers for job retention (Berryhill, 2021). The researcher sought to understand the threats to principal longevity through a phenomenological research study investigating and collecting data on principals lived experiences and their perceptions regarding job satisfaction, school context, and autonomous decision-making.

The study included 52 elementary school principals. Twenty-nine served at schools in impoverished communities receiving federal funding, and 23 served at schools in more affluent communities. School sizes ranged from 300 students to over 1,250 students.

The research study was important to determine why principals were leaving their school posts, as the district exceeded the nation's average principal turnover. How do job satisfaction, school context, and autonomy play a role in the retention of principals? The principal retention data were then categorized by positive, negative, and mooring (or stabilizing) retention factors through the Push-Pull-Mooring (PPM) theory (Heffernan, 2020). The PPM theory helps us understand why people change locations or permanently leave positions.

Push-Pull-Mooring theory is defined by the push being largely negative factors causing dissatisfaction, the pull being generally positive factors or new opportunity, and the mooring factors acting as stabilizers that outweigh the push or pull factors and encourage a person to stay in place (Berryhill, 2021).

Survey responses related to job satisfaction indicated that principals were satisfied with being instructional leaders, having some autonomy (they want more) to make decisions for what is suitable for their schools, creating and nurturing relationships with their staff, students, families, and school communities, and cultivating growth with their students. They also expressed satisfaction with personnel who were assigned to their school in support roles, including the assistant superintendent.

However, the principals were dissatisfied with the lack of support coming from district supervisors and departments. Principals stated the desire for district staff to be more knowledgeable about school-based leadership before making district decisions that impacted schools. They felt overwhelmed with compliance-driven tasks, workload expectations, personnel issues, lack of funding and resources, and being disrespected by district personnel and parents. They felt salaries were not comparable to other jobs with similar qualifications. A general concern was the impact stress levels had on families and themselves.

School contextual factors vary significantly from one school to the next (i.e., socioeconomics, diversity of students, size of the population, and special programs) and impact how district initiatives are implemented. Grissom and Bartanen (2019) found that school contextual factors can predict principal turnover. Regarding the survey questions about school context, principals focused on wanting additional support for their school from district staff, the need for more autonomous decision-making, flexibility with allocations, and additional technology.

Principal responses for autonomous decision-making clearly emphasized their need for autonomy around instructional practices, school budgets, use of allocations, and determining programmatic moves for students. Principal participants further noted they wanted input into district decision-making that impacted their school. They also believe personnel in district departments have room for growth in understanding systems that support school principals. There was a strong interest in a systematic principal feedback loop allowing current principals to input their needs and share their perceptions.

Together, district leaders and principals could build collaborative relationships to accomplish the goals of the schools addressing the factors impacting principal turnover and retention. Seeking out solutions in a collaborative manner with school districts will lead to less stress and principal turnover. In conclusion, principals in the district of study enjoyed being principals and were passionate about their work. The findings suggest that principals want a collaborative partnership with the district that allows them more autonomous decision-making to meet the unique needs of their school community.

SUPPORTIVE PRACTICES FOR NOVICE PRINCIPALS

The growing turnover rates of K–12 principals have been a concern since before the country faced the coronavirus outbreak; one in five principals leave their school each year (Zalaznick, 2020). The second study mentioned above investigated the practices of the central Florida school district for supporting new principals who encounter different situations and social conditions in their assigned schools, making it essential for district leadership to ease these challenges by providing support before and after their appointment (Gates et at., 2019).

The phenomenological study, *Supportive practices for novice principals*, was completed through semistructured interviews of two school district administrators and several focus groups with new principals (Steinacker, 2022). Interviews with the school district administrators were completed to gain an understanding of the school district's perception of the needs and current supports provided to new principals during the first three years of their principalship. Conducting focus groups with the new principals provided the opportunity to share their experiences in their own words and provide details of the support they were provided since becoming a principal.

At the time of the study, the school district had 15 new elementary principals hired since January 1, 2019. Ten of them participated in focus groups that were made up of three to five participants. The participants' experiences as a principal ranged from less than six months to three years.

The semistructured interviews of the school district administrators revealed that the school district of the study had an extensive process for selecting individuals for their principal pool and had a principal pipeline. The Preparing New Principal Program (PNPP) was an essential component of the principal pipeline.

When individuals were selected for the principal pool, they entered the PNPP. This program guided individuals through various experiences related to the principal leadership standards, allowing them to earn their principal certification. These principal pipeline components were provided before an individual entered their first principalship. Study findings showed that the support provided once hired as a new principal was mainly a principal mentor and monthly principal meetings.

The findings from these focus groups confirmed that prior to becoming principals, each had completed the PNPP, which provided them with various experiences in preparation for becoming a principal. However, participants shared that they needed more training that prepared them for the challenges they faced during their first year, which included understanding the established culture and routines of their new school, creating a partnership with their assistant principal, navigating the plethora of new information, and how to let go of what they found familiar. Half the participants experienced these challenges during the COVID pandemic, so the support they received was the same provided to all principals, even those with many years of experience.

The findings from the focus groups showed that nine of the ten new principals were assigned a principal mentor. The three participants who were in their first year or first six months of their principalship were also assigned a Gallup Strengths Coach, and the two who were assigned to academically struggling schools also were given a retired principal as a mentor.

There was no consistency in the level of support received from the principal mentors. Some mentors made initial contact and then failed to follow up, some only sent text messages, and a third of the mentors regularly scheduled meetings. Study participants also relied on the principals they previously worked under for guidance and support; for one study participant, this was her only source of mentoring.

A pilot program had been implemented within the last year specifically developed to support new principals. The New Elementary Principal Network (NEPN) included monthly meetings focused on essential learning and networking opportunities. During their meetings, the new principal group also engaged in collaborative discussions around Problems of Practice, which provided the new principals with strategies they could use to solve similar problems in the future.

The focus group findings also showed that participants received support through monthly district principal meetings. However, it was only when novice principals were invited to participate in NEPN that they felt they received beneficial support. Topics discussed at the NEPN meetings were relevant to what study participants were experiencing in their new role, and the similarities in these experiences gave participants a sense that they were not alone. One of the participants shared that she had felt very lonely when becoming a principal, and now she had colleagues who shared common concerns.

The focus group participants were asked to share what they wished they had known before they became a principal and what training would have helped them. The number one response was how to manage the pressure of the job. One participant simply said she was unprepared for the weight of it all. Additional responses discussed included managing daily tasks, feeling lonely, overwhelmed, and navigating staff who negatively influenced the school culture.

The district in this study had an extensive application process for an individual to enter the principal pool through an established principal pipeline; however, the school district's limited succession planning did little to ensure the optimal applicant was hired to replace a principal. The findings from the focus group showed that the most impactful support provided to the new principals was the establishment of the NEPN.

In conclusion, new principals are confronted by many challenges during their first years, many of which are unanticipated. They often experience anxiety, frustration, and professional isolation during their first year, potentially leading them to leave after only one year (Salazar, 2020). The increasing rate of principal turnover makes it necessary for school systems to rethink how they support new principals to successfully meet the mounting demands of improving teaching and learning and raising student achievement (Levin et al., 2019). Taking a closer look at the NEPN as a potential solution for retaining school leaders is worthwhile, but first, let us consider networking as a leadership skill.

NETWORKING AS A LEADERSHIP SKILL

As postulated in this book, networking is becoming an integral function of sustaining today's organizations and thus a critical leadership skill. As such, network thinking will be part of the next generation of leadership skills necessary to manage schools that must adapt and change with societal expectations. Snyder and Snyder (2021) promote network perspectives and practices that allow leaders to "develop an organization's resilience, its energy, and innovative practices that adapt work quickly in emerging and challenging conditions" (p. 3).

Karolyn Snyder's chapter in this book gives a detailed account of the history and principles of networks based on the science of networks. The goal is to create systems that empower and motivate leaders to want to lead. If a district hopes to retain effective principals in positions, a different mode of support is necessary. In the two previous studies highlighted in this chapter, school leaders clearly state the need for more strategic and robust support from their supervisors and the district office. A network model links individuals in a highly motivating, collaborative atmosphere for personal and group development (Snyder & Snyder, 2021).

Districts would be wise to focus on facilitating principals' networks to respond to the emerging challenges and opportunities of today's school leaders. Traditional top-down personal and professional support models are inadequate for today's dynamic, systems-driven learning environments.

A PRINCIPAL NETWORK SUCCESS STORY

A primary goal of every organization is to develop and retain leadership. If that is the case, we must consider leadership skills and well-being that address the increasingly complex pressures of the job of being a leader. Not surprisingly, as we have explored thus far in this chapter, the need for more support and understanding of what motivates principals to stay committed to their roles is a critical area of study.

Principals are unique individuals, but all are motivated to manage change, increase mastery levels of staff, build community connections, and provide rigorous and relevant learning opportunities for all students. The success of principals depends to a large degree on various district structures of support as they learn and grow.

Research indicates that districts play a crucial role in providing the supporting structures and systems that build capacity in school leaders to overcome challenges (Ford et al., 2020). Darling-Hammond et al. (2021) recently synthesized the literature on what it takes to build capacity in young leaders to positively impact student and teacher outcomes. According to her findings, exemplary district programs provide learning opportunities to apply learning in practice, focus on improving instruction, and create ways to collaborate through cohorts or networking structures.

In a review of research, Anderson and Young (2018) capture critical elements of what makes a school district effective. Three domains highlight where districts should focus: student learning and instructional practices, the structures and management of the organization, and the support and leadership of the people in schools and districts. Across the domains, a district's ability to foster positive self-efficacy in principals increases the capacity to accomplish the goals and mission of the schools and district. District staff development provides support so that individuals believe they are capable, autonomous, and part of the leadership system.

Anderson and Young's (2018) research defines what district support should look like for school leaders, but they state that districts have not changed how they operate in decades, including how they provide support for school leaders. Basically, districts focus on "top down" (hierarchical) approaches largely based on pressures of accountability and traditional management strategies.

A different approach in support of school leaders would provide an opportunity to learn vicariously with other principals in a peer-to-peer network. Learning opportunities that allow for self-directed learning and grappling with one's capabilities and feelings of self-efficacy are more aligned with what principals say they need.

Snyder and Snyder (2021) point out that after decades of studying ways to improve organizations, there is compelling evidence that networks and network thinking are the critical missing leadership skills that will make schools sustainable in adaptation, innovation, and high performance. Regarding networks, the authors state, "This is a story about human energy and how it can be systemically supported and unleashed in organizations to continually adapt to emerging challenges and opportunities" (Snyder & Snyder, 2021, p. 4). The recommendation is to bring awareness to the power of networking as a sustainable feature of leadership development and support.

The New Elementary Principal Network was designed to provide novice principals with the kind of district support mentioned in the current literature on school leadership and networking. It was an initiative started in a central Florida school district by the assistant superintendent based on perceived needs for support and professional development of principals in their first three years of leading a school. The NEPN is a network prototype providing novice principals a place to learn, reflect, and collaborate and where self-efficacy and learning about leadership can flourish through the intellectual and emotional support of peers.

What networks have to offer is a systemic way of building a culture that is highly responsive to the needs of the individual. At the same time, networking creates a connected system across interdependent schools. All networks advance the district's primary goal of providing families and students with the best possible educational experience.

To that end, the district can take the lead in organizing, fostering, and sustaining network systems. Currently, school districts need to see building networks as part of the mainstream work of developing and retaining school principals. If we hope to impact the longevity of principals, networks and the skill of networking as a leader are next-generation initiatives in the effort to transform schools into sustainable systems.

The NEPN is a network experience based on an organic learning process driven by novice principals who face systemic challenges. Did the NEPN deliver on promises to enhance the self-efficacy of principals, create bonds of trust, build knowledge, and provide a safe environment to learn and grow? The answer is a resounding YES! Results of several measures suggest a positive change in all participants of the program.

The two measures used to determine the impact of the NEPN program on novice principals included the Principals' Sense of Efficacy Scale (PSES) and an informal measure of professional school and district networks. Both measures were pre-post and analyzed for changes across individuals and the group. The PSES was developed by Tschannen-Moran and Gareis (2004) and is an accepted assessment of a leader's self-efficacy.

Tschannen-Moran (2022) defined self-efficacy within the context of school leaders' beliefs of how capable they are of making a difference in leading schools and effectively managing the complexity of the role. The positive impact of the NEPN program was seen in the analysis of PSES results. Changes in both the mean total score and individual items suggest a positive trajectory in self-efficacy in all participants over the year-long program. The individual item that showed the highest overall change from pre to post was, "As a principal, to what extent can you manage change in your school?"

The second survey principals participated in was an informal measure to capture critical school-based and district-based people in their network. The same survey was administered pre-post to determine changes. The tool asked them to list the names of those who have most frequently helped with advice or answered questions related to their job and then to indicate the kind of help given, for example, technical, problem-solving, knowledge/information, and emotional support. Participants separately listed school-based and district-based network connections. The objective of this informal activity was to see if networks expanded and changed.

The self-reflection tool measuring network size revealed that principal networks practically doubled for all but one participant. Two principals tripled the number of people that they frequently go to for various forms of support. The NEPN created strong bonds allowing once-isolated principals to feel a sense of belonging to a network. The sense of togetherness evolved around both the need for emotional support and the need for knowledge and problem-solving.

These measures highlight the need for a systemic approach to professional development and support of novice principals that includes networking and network thinking. Districts focusing on knowing what principals value and the relationships principals need to improve leadership competencies and self-efficacy will position themselves to retain principals and build the entire organization's capacity.

A CALL TO ACTION

The sustainability of schooling as we know it today is threatened by a looming exodus of school leaders. In a recently published article, the principalship was described as a position with all the responsibility and none of the power (Greene, 2022). The author notes that the desire to be a school leader has been diminishing along with teaching due to the factors addressed in this chapter.

After considering the results of three recent studies in a central Florida school district, one can conclude that systems of support and networks for collaboration are lacking. Compliance-driven professional development is not the solution. In this same district, an innovative approach to a natural support system has evolved. Early results show promise that this organic model of the New Elementary Principal Network delivers on the notion that networks offer a systemic way of building a culture that is highly responsive to the needs of the individual and, at the same time, the whole system.

Addressing the issue of principal sustainability will become a focus for school districts across the nation. Building networks of support with organically created systems of collaboration will offer the promise of a new way of work for our school leaders and preserve the sustainability of schooling. The time has come for district leaders to engage with principals in a new way of work.

REFERENCES

Anderson, E., & Young, M. D. (2018). If they knew then what we know now, why haven't things changed? An examination of district effectiveness research. *Frontiers in Education*, 3(87), 1–20.

Babo, G., & Petty, D. (2019). The influence of a principal's length of service and school socioeconomic classification on teacher retention rates in New Jersey middle schools. *Journal of Leadership and Instruction*, 18(1), 8–11.

Berryhill, T. (2021, March). *Factors impacting elementary retention: job satisfaction, school context, and autonomous decision-making* (Doctoral dissertation). Saint Leo University. ProQuest Dissertations & Theses Global.

Bradley, K., & Levin, S. (2019). Understanding and addressing principal turnover. National Association of Secondary School Principals. https://www.nassp.org/2019/06/05/understanding-and-addressing-principal-turnover/

Darling-Hammond, L., Wechsler, M. E., Levin, S., Leung-Gagne, M., & Tozer, S. (2022). Developing effective principals: What kind of learning matters? [Report]. Learning Policy Institute. https://doi.org/10.54300/641.201

Fabel, L. (2016). The enormous effort to retain principals in Dallas. Teach for America. https://www.teachforamerica.org/one-day/magazine/the-enormous-efforts-to-retain-young-principals-in-dallas

Ford, T. G., Lavigne, A. L., Fiegener, A. M., & Si, S. (2020). Understanding district support for leader development and success in the accountability era: A review of the literature using social-cognitive theories of motivation. *Review of Educational Research*, 90(2), 264–307.

Gates, S., Baird, M., Master, B., & Chavez-Herrerias, E. (2019). *Principal pipelines: A feasible, affordable, and effective way for districts to improve schools*. RAND Corporation.

Greene, P. (2022). The public school problem that we're not talking about. Forbes Education. https://www.forbes.com/sites/petergreene/2022/07/17/the-public-school-problem-that-were-not-talking-about/?sh=50e897c57407

Grissom, J., & Bartanen, B. (2019). Principal effectiveness and principal turnover. *Education Finance and Policy*, 14(3), 355–382.

Heffernan, A. (2020). Retaining Australia's school leaders in 'challenging' contexts: The importance of personal relationships in principal turnover decisions. *International Journal of Educational Research*, 105, 1–9.

Henry, G., & Harbatkin, E. (2019). *Turnover at the top: Estimating the effects of principal turnover on student, teacher, and school outcomes*. Annenberg Institute at Brown University.

Levin, S., Bradley, K., & Scott, C. (2019). Principal turnover: Insights from current principals. *Learning Policy Institute*, National Association of Secondary School Principals.

McMurdock, M. (2022). School leader crisis: overwhelmed by mounting mental health issues and public distrust, a 'mass exodus' of principals could be coming. The74 (February 20, 2022). https://www.the74million.org/article/school-leaders-crisis-overwhelmed-by-mounting-mental-health-issues-public-distrust-mass-exodus-of-principals-could-be-coming/

National Association of Elementary School Principals. (2021). What we learned from elementary school principals about changes to schools and the profession emerging from 2020–2021. https://www.naesp.org/resource/leaders-we-need-now/

National Association of Secondary School Principals. (2017). Position statement: Principal shortage. (March 27, 2017). https://www.nassp.org/principal-shortage/

National Association of Secondary School Principals. (2022). NASSP survey signals a looming mass exodus of principals from schools. (December 8, 2021). https://www.nassp.org/news/nassp-survey-signals-a-looming-mass-exodus-of-principals-from-schools/

Ruggirello, A. (2022). New research points to a looming principal shortage. The Wallace Foundation. (February 23, 2022).

Salazar, A. (2020). *A phenomenology: Novice principals' perception of early challenges, best practices, strategies, and support systems* (Doctoral dissertation). San Diego State University.

Snyder, K. J., & Snyder, K. (2021). The role of human network systems for leading sustainable quality in organisations. In *Proceedings of the 27th Annual Conference, International Sustainable Development Research Society: Accelerating the progress towards the 2030 SDGs in times of crisis*. Östersund: annual conference international sustainable development society. (1997–2016).

Steinacker, C. (2022). *Supportive practices for novice Principals* (Doctoral dissertation). Saint Leo University.
Superville, D. (2022). Principals may be dissatisfied. That doesn't mean they're leaving. *Education Week.* (May 23, 2022).
Tschannen-Moran, M., & Gareis, C. (2004). Principals sense of efficacy: Assessing a promising construct. *Journal of Educational Administration*, 42, 573–585.
Tschannen-Moran, M. (2022). Principal's sense of self-efficacy. Research tools: Megan Tschannen-Moran website. https://mxtsch.pages.wm.edu/research-tools/
Tyre, P. (2015). Why do more than half of the principals quit after five years? The Hechinger Report. https://hechingerreport.org/why-do-more-than-half-of-principals-quit-after-five-years/
Woo, A., & Steiner, E. D. (2021). The well-being of secondary school principals one year into the covid-19 pandemic. RAND Corporation. https://www.rand.org/pubs/research_reports/RRA827-6.html
Zalaznick, Matt. (2020). Why principal turnover is alarming education experts. *District Administration.* May 15. https://districtadministration.com/why-principal-turnover-is-alarming-education-experts/

Chapter 4

Systems Thinking Training and School District Transformation

John Mann

Education is facing unusual times. A mass exodus of administrators is likely to happen, and fewer people are entering the profession (Scanga & Sedlack, 2023). If successful principals leave, it will create an irreplaceable experience gap for public schools, which holds a special place in creating the fabric of our nation. There is a constant need for quality public schools in every district in the United States. With that in mind, it is imperative that new and experienced administrators are prepared properly with a new mindset to find success in the current landscape.

Educators need the school district and individual schools within it to create a sense of hope through a clear vision and a dedication to high-level training for all administrators. This very thing occurred in Pasco County, Florida, 27 years ago with the creation of three crucial training programs focused on systems thinking and quality management that are still highly relevant today. As Henry Glassie stated, "history is not the past but a map of the past, drawn from a particular point of view, to be useful to the modern traveler" (History Quotes, 2019).

According to a former assistant superintendent of schools, "Pasco County was a district dedicated to discovering and studying the most valuable research studies to impact instruction, positive change, and school leadership. Pasco County wanted the best research to drive change by encouraging creativity." Pasco County schools met its match with a new professor in education at the University of South Florida who was ready to pilot a new training program to develop schools from a systems view. The idea was to train all principals and district administrators in systems thinking and continuous progress. Pasco County seemed like a perfect fit.

The 27-year journey and commitment to develop and lead school districts from a systems perspective in Pasco County was born. Over time, details of the approach were refined to meet the continuing needs of the district. The continuous improvement of strategies also reflected a deepening understanding of the complexity of leading education from a systems perspective.

The first of the three crucial programs was called Managing Productive Schools (MPS), which lasted from 1986 to 1997. MPS, a 25-day program, provided a collaborative systems approach to leading and learning with a robust collection of tools to accomplish the district's vision. After going through a training program, pairs of trainers led cadres to develop a common language, tools, and vision (Snyder & Anderson, 1986).

The follow-up program, Leadership for Sustainable School Development (LSSD), from 2006 to 2013, highlighted a collaborative, systems thinking approach to school leadership that was the cornerstone of MPS, but it added an emphasis on the tenets of quality management and global connectedness and sustainability (Snyder et al., 2008).

The third program, Global Partnership Program (GPP), was in place from 2008 to 2012 (Snyder et al., 2010). The purpose of the GPP was to create a safe environment for educators and students from different countries to meet, work, and grow together. Together, these three programs created a space for a deep understanding of collaborative systems and the power of systems thinking. They allowed an entire system to move progressively and sustainably forward.

In this chapter, interviews with the expert district trainers provide crucial insights into the three programs, reflecting and highlighting the reasons for their successes. The leaders interviewed held many positions, including assistant principal, principal, director, and assistant superintendent, within the district over the time of implementation of training, and they contributed greatly to the important story. The article's researcher was involved in every level of the training and also held all the leadership positions and shared insights from those perspectives.

Implementing the systems, tools, and philosophy of MPS, LSSD, and GPP changed the trajectory of Pasco County, impacting its overall culture. It changed the path by bringing all administrators together with expert trainers who gave them a sense of purpose and professional community. The administrators had the opportunity to practice their new skills and had all tools necessary to be successful. This story focuses on a consistent district vision of collaborative systems thinking that was successful because leaders welcomed it and had enough resources and expert guidance to support the district-wide staff development initiative.

MANAGING PRODUCTIVE SCHOOLS
- MPS (1986 TO 1997)

In January 1986, a pilot group of administrators started their MPS journey in a conference room at a rural high school in Pasco County. "The program looked like something that we would be interested in and would complement what we were doing, but it was not a definite yes that we would continue after the first group. I invited interested principals and assistant principals from all levels to form the pilot cadre to gauge their reactions. They are the ones that said that this training program gave them a whole picture of how to improve their schools. It was a definite yes!" (Former Assistant Superintendent of Schools).

A brand-new assistant principal at the rural high school stood outside the conference room, looking in through the small window. The initial MPS training was inside, just beyond his reach. Standing outside the training room was torture because of the progressive nature of the shared ideas and his love of professional development. Having just completed his doctorate at a major university, he realized this training was different and unique. It was something to which he had not been exposed, and he knew it was invaluable.

The purpose of the MPS training program was to provide the philosophical foundation, tools, and practical experience to lead a collaborative systems-driven school, department, or district (Snyder, 2007). A systems model was developed that helped leaders think differently about leading and managing schools. In-depth work was being done on how "systems thinking helps principals move their schools beyond traditions of worker isolation to develop work cultures of shared purpose and meaning, staff collaboration and interdependent work units" (Snyder & Snyder, 1996, p. 68).

When discussing MPS, Snyder and Anderson (1986) shared that "a systems approach to school management and organization provides a conceptual framework for developing a new paradigm. Schooling practices will become increasingly integrated as they focus on specific goals and working collaboratively" (p. 28).

The foundation for the initial training was based on extensive research in several areas of leadership and a systems approach to school improvement, outlined in the book *Managing Productive Schools: Toward an Ecology* (Snyder & Anderson, 1986). It was the first time everything was put together in one training that encouraged administrators to work in a collaborative way and not attempt to manage in isolation. It was a huge undertaking and would end up being a 25-day-long training over two years (Giella & Stanfill, 1996).

Robert H. Anderson positively impacted the training through his addition of Continuous Progress, a multiage and team-teaching approach to the curriculum and instruction structures that changed processes and had a meaningful impact on the school district and the instructional philosophy for students. The three educators, Karolyn J. Snyder, Robert H. Anderson, and Mary Giella, contributed significantly to how MPS was delivered and became critical learning community members.

After the pilot program ended, and it was determined that the training would continue, several new and voluntary cadres of administrators were started. With the addition of the new administrators, there began a positive seismic disruption in how things were done in the schools and district. MPS evolved into a training initiative that all administrators attended, and it lasted 11 years. Each cadre not only had a unique color but also a name, shirts, and songs, which created a unique identity for each group. It also had a positive impact on the district as a whole.

The impact of MPS training in the schools sent a ripple through the district. For the first time, staff realized that they had a voice and that their voice counted. An interview respondent noted that it helped get people beyond the daily work of running a school and gave them a different perspective, with a shared vision, language, experience, tools, and skills. People started to realize that everyone was important and that amazing ideas came not only from teachers but also from instructional aides and administrative assistants.

Schools were improved through an approach in which administrators learned "the integration, interdependence, and cohesiveness of school work systems (which) stimulate sustainable growth over time" (Snyder, 2008). They also learned that in order to succeed in a systems approach to leadership, administrators must keep the organization's primary purpose at the forefront of their actions. Schools developed practical and carefully thought-out vision statements and goals that directed the work of the schools. The staff expected accountability but was willing to pitch in and assist to make it happen.

The change in research practices had a direct impact on the district trends. MPS supported the district's dedication to best research practices. Evidence of this was the implementation of strategies around the Continuous Progress approach. It was a multiage, nongraded system design that encouraged students to work at their own levels regardless of age. The increase in teaming and team teaching increased the level of instruction by taking advantage of teachers' strengths.

In elementary schools, almost all students were served in K–2 or 3–5 teams through a curriculum designed and delivered by teachers working together to create the best learning environment for each child. At the beginning of the school year, it was not unusual to see second-grade students welcoming and assisting kindergarten students. The transition for our newest students was heartwarming as students helped every new person adapt to the team.

MPS often provided a structure on which to hang other superb ideas and training that previously seemed to exist in isolation. A solid conceptual framework makes it easy to see where everything fits and provides greater clarification of purpose and intent. The training design allowed participants to learn why something was important, be exposed to new skills, and practice them in a training session before practicing them in the field. It was understood that all discussion was encouraged as long as it was connected to research and excellent practice. The training was organized around six major subsystems and the areas highlighted in each section (see Figure 4.1).

Many administrators understood the importance of school culture but had no way to address or measure it. This was rectified through the introduction in MPS training with the critical tool called the School Work Culture Profile (SWCP), which "measures work culture development around four

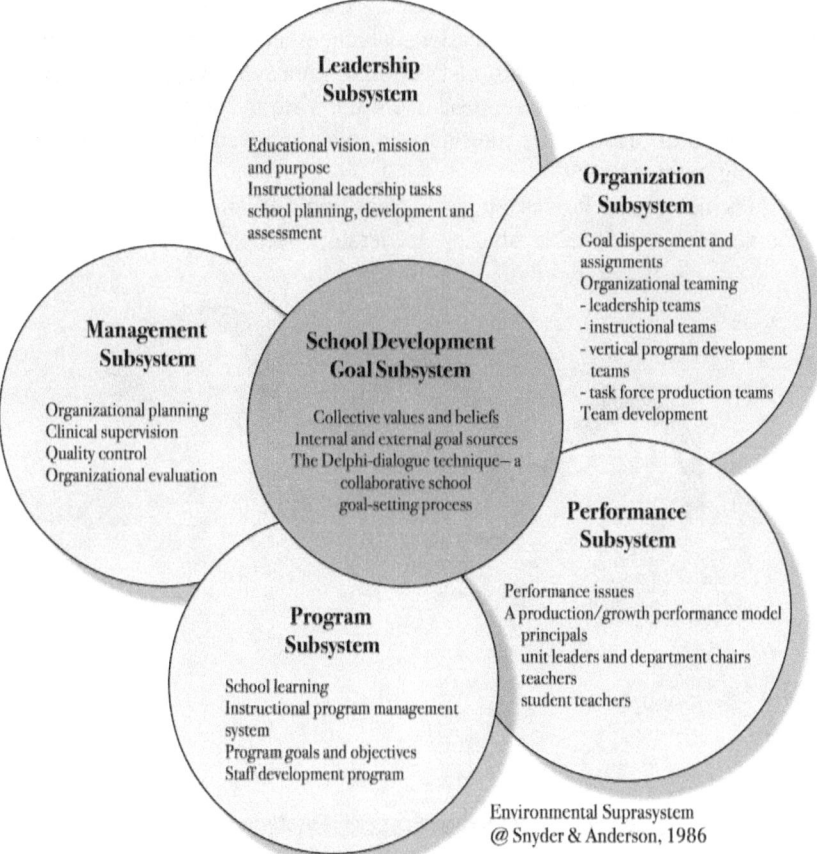

Figure 4.1. Managing Productive Schools Model

subdomains: planning, program development, staff development, and assessment. The instrument measures the extent of worker involvement in organizational practice" (Snyder et al., 2006, p. 189). The model (Figure 4.2) has four subdomains and ten competencies.

"Productive schools, as well as other productive organizations in society, have characteristics which set them apart from less effective places of work. This instrument is designed to help you analyze the culture in your school in relation to ideal work patterns" (Snyder, 1988, p. 71). The training confirmed that the SWCP measures the single factor of school work culture as a living system in a study of the teachers in 25 schools. The study differentiated high-performing work cultures from low ones (Parkinson, 1990). It is a tool that is still relevant today and should be reviewed and used.

The 25-day training program, spread over two years, was unique to the district and the state. The time together created a closeness that is not always possible to establish in a larger district. It also brought recognition from the Florida Department of Education, which asked for many new training programs about systems and instructional improvement (Snyder, 2007). Interviewees noted that the requests from the state to train others brought a special sense of pride to the interviewees, who believed they were a part of something extraordinary.

It does not mean it was an easy transition for all administrators, and everyone was comfortable sharing leadership. According to an interview

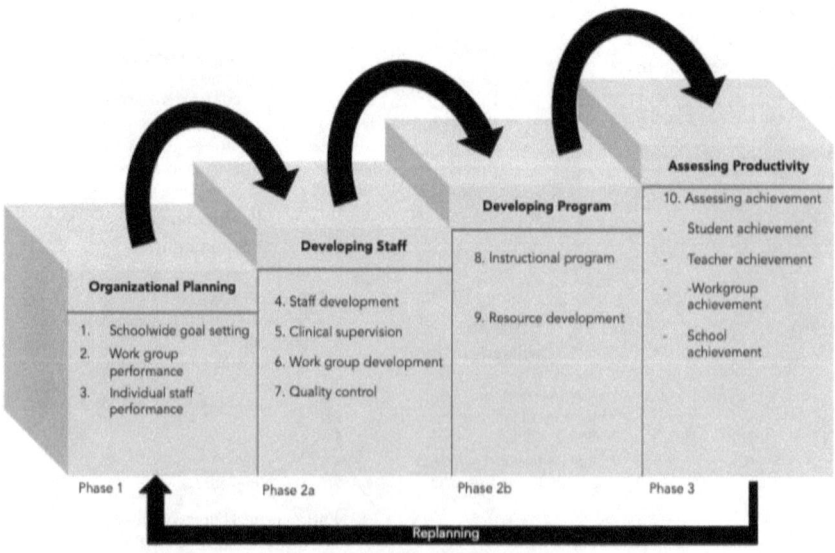

Figure 4.2. School Work Culture Profile Model

respondent, some initially resistant people became convinced by observing and visiting other schools and seeing their success. Others realized through feeder pattern meetings that the schools participating in a more cooperative and collaborative work environment were more successful. After a collaborative schoolwide goal-setting session, one teacher asked if we could go back to being told what to do because it was a lot of pressure to help guide a school.

While a small group of district and school holdouts tried to wait out the initiative, their training time finally arrived. The group decided they would be the best cadre and chose to be known as the Black Diamonds. Though it was not a piece of cake for them, their struggle produced a mind shift and their own success stories.

According to one interviewee, the training and work in the schools were meaningful because MPS helped her problem-solve positively and collaboratively. It impacted and changed her life personally and professionally. Clearly, the focus on culture, climate, and relationships was making workplaces happier. "Since we now understand that schools are not machines to be run and fixed when needed, educators need fresh perspectives for exploring schools as natural living systems that grow and adapt routinely to changing conditions" (Snyder, 2023, p. 5).

In summary, many critical big ideas were evident through the implementation and impact of MPS. Committing to district-wide administrative training takes vision, commitment, support, and participation of key personnel, and courage. Creating and sharing a common vocabulary about the leadership concepts deemed important based on the research and the use of experts adds credibility to the training. Timing for the rollout of training must be considered as well as a clear idea of how to adjust implementation expectations.

The training must be well-planned, interactive, and participatory, focusing on how adults best learn. Using a train-the-trainer model highlights that a leader not only has a duty to their school but also to all schools through professional development. Taking risks supported by your vision is worthwhile as long as one remembers there are no silver bullets. Lastly, have fun during training. It will carry over to the workplace!

KEYS TO REMEMBER

- Develop an agreed-upon vision.
- Common language and experiences should come out of the training.
- Develop a collaborative approach to decision-making and goal setting.

- Have a set of tools to accomplish collaboratively determined goals.
- Positive relational leadership is not transactional.
- A story sharing the success or importance of one's school allows stakeholders to connect emotionally; be a storyteller.
- Have fun!

LEADERSHIP FOR SUSTAINABLE SCHOOL DEVELOPMENT (2006 TO 2013)

In 2006, Max Ramos, the first director of leadership development in Pasco County, approached Karolyn Snyder after attending one of her presentations. With the support of the new superintendent, he asked her to create follow-up training for Managing Productive Schools. The ten-year gap between MPS and LSSD created by leadership changes and different areas of focus at the highest level left a void in some leaders' understanding of the power of a collaborative systemic approach to schooling. The training finally started with a group of experienced MPS trainers participating in the first trainer training for LSSD.

Snyder agreed to design, lead, and facilitate the new 11-day training. One significant difference in the development and delivery of LSSD was how it was done collaboratively, with a district design team comprised of veteran trainers and professional development specialists. The design team evolved during the training cycle, and there was a review and adjustments made after every cadre finished their training. Working with a group of professionals with the same goal of creating a training program focused on systems thinking was exciting. The updated and streamlined training met the new training needs of the district.

The training days were organized under five headings, making up the LSSD training program. They were:

- Day 1 - Analyzing the Global Context of Schooling
- Day 2 - Leading Through Technology
- Day 3 - A Systemic Orientation to School Development
- Day 4 - Conducting a School Case Study
- Day 5 - Goal Setting for School Development
- Day 6 - School-Wide Work Teams
- Day 7 - Professional Learning Communities
- Day 8 - Organization of Student Learning Communities
- Day 9 - The 21st Century Student Learning System

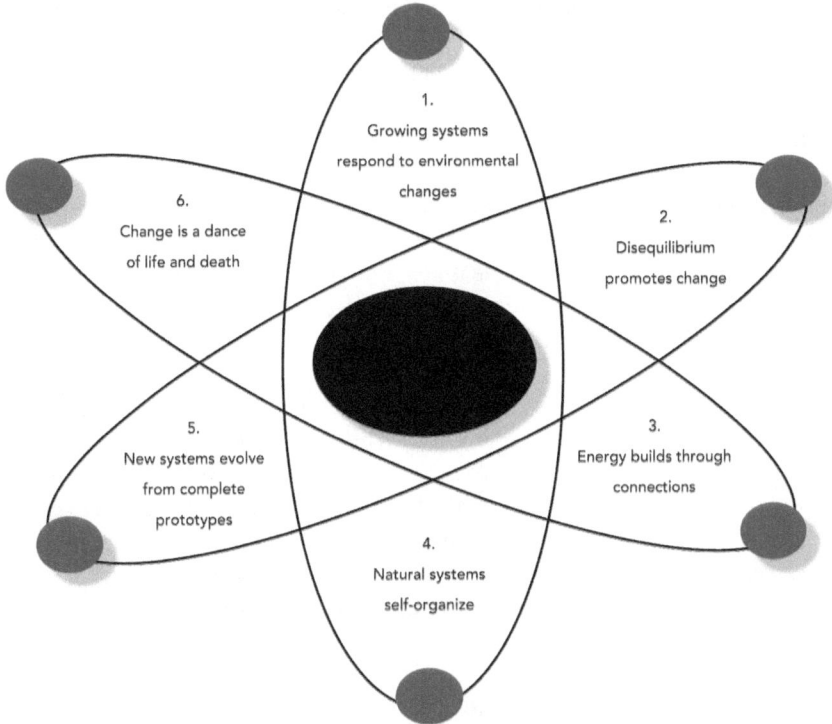

Figure 4.3. Atomic Model: Living on the Edge of Chaos (Snyder et al., 2008, p. 79).

- Day 10 - Benchmarking Progress
- Day 11 - Reporting the Effects of LSSD Training (Snyder, 2012)

The purpose of the LSSD program was to build leadership capacities to stimulate sustainable school development that prepares youth for success in a global age of sustainable living and working (Snyder, 1988). For administrators trained in a collaborative systems approach during MPS, it boosted their skills and assisted in refocusing on a comprehensive and systemic approach for each school, department, and district. A new book, *Living on the Edge of Chaos: Leading Schools into the Global Age*, was used to support the training materials (Snyder et al., 2006).

LSSD, through the introduction of the Atomic Model: Living on the Edge of Chaos, pushed the administrators to think differently and test what they believed about traditional leadership theory. The model contained six dimensions.

Exploring each dimension of the model challenged participants and their thinking. Acknowledging that powerful outside forces impact our daily lives was significant, but working together to acquire tools to influence those forces benefited everyone's growth (Snyder et al., 2008, pp. 79–80). It was liberating for some leaders and scary for others when they understood they needed to embrace disequilibrium instead of always trying to be a fixer. The idea itself created disequilibrium.

The powerful idea shared during training that natural systems self-organize and that school leadership resistance is a disservice to education forced deep discussions of what strategies were needed. The dimension that stated that change was a dance of life and death caught everyone's attention. Many outdated structures and procedures sometimes need to be ended for better ideas to grow and flourish, thus the need for things to die to make way for growth (Snyder et al., 2008).

Just as some dimensions of the model stretched thinking tremendously, some felt more attuned to past training. The LSSD cadres generally understood the power and importance of relationships, and the stronger the connections developed, the more the organization is able to respond to challenges, as well as create new and evolving systems made up of prototypes encouraging experimentation that fit the district premise of encouraging progressive work (Snyder et al., 2008). Working from the model about chaos was a critical addition to LSSD training.

All administrators in the district were trained, with new administrators added to the cadres scheduled later in the training cycle. In the planning for LSSD cadres, there was consideration for having various school-based principals and assistant principals at different levels balanced with instructional and noninstructional district administrators. The personalities of the trainers and cadre members were also considered in determining the groups, which helped create a foundation for positive and trusting relationships. It allowed leaders to feel comfortable approaching and working with people with whom they would not typically be associated.

The reduction in face-to-face training days meant careful planning was needed to ensure every minute of the day was leveraged and appropriate follow-up activities were conducted back in the participants' worksites. A day exploring all the latest advances in educational technology was added to the training cycle. We invited people from within the cadres, as well as experts in the field, to share their successes and knowledge. Just as during MPS training, cadres had names, colors, and songs to add to the culture and comradery.

There was an immediate response in the schools. More experienced administrators trained in MPS immediately started using more collaborative and inclusive skills again. There had been some regression to old practices, so LSSD substantially impacted attention to culture and climate.

> **KEYS TO REMEMBER**
>
> - The diversity of the training groups increased understanding of each other's challenges and abilities while contributing to a positive district culture.
> - Understanding the power of networks and systems supports our schools' success.
> - A district commitment in which all administrators work toward the same vision unifies.
> - It is essential to build on individual and district strengths and utilize the district's history with MPS to develop new success stories.

The interviewees noted that day 11 of LSSD allowed people to share their stories and how they had applied what they learned. It was a powerful and enjoyable day.

LSSD assisted our school leaders in understanding the importance of leading a living system versus a system based on compliance. A former assistant superintendent remarked, "it is important to understand and work with and around things thrown at us by the legislature. The only way to be successful is to understand and be fully committed to your vision."

In summary, many critical big ideas were evident throughout the implementation and impact of LSSD. Expanding the training design team was a real positive, making sure they tapped into excellent research with the help of experts. The positive reinforcement through celebrating the accomplishments of each cadre was beneficial and rewarding and, because of the groups' diversity, added a deeper understanding of each leader's challenges and abilities. Giving administrators a solid set of tools was beneficial, as was helping them think with a futuristic perspective.

It was critical to push people's thinking by studying and applying the chaos model while also showing respect for the participants through the training design and delivery. Reestablishing one training for all administrators based on collaborative systems thinking unified the district.

GLOBAL PARTNERSHIP PROGRAM
– GPP (2008 TO 2012)

The purpose of the GPP program was to build meaningful global relationships among educators and students while developing cultural and academic awareness in a safe and accessible environment. The GPP is one of the most exciting and challenging programs the leadership director has ever been associated with. It was exciting because the students and teachers did some extraordinary work. It was challenging because of the differences in first languages, time zones, cultures, and school expectations.

The GPP would not have been possible without the invitation and support of International Schools Connection (ISC) (Snyder et al., 2006), which has "as its mission to help school and district leaders develop their schools as Global Learning Centers, where students become global citizens over time " (Snyder et al., 2010, p. 6). The ISC had long-standing relationships with school districts in Sweden and China and provided the district contacts and structures. After the initial three-continent partnership concluded, classes in Pasco were matched with classes in Spain, Italy, and Ireland.

The GPP was successful because of the ISC and the use of the Global Learning Center Benchmarks as the guideposts for the work. The benchmarks have two parts, one in creating a learning environment for students and the second in preparing for success in a global environment. Some keys to success were providing opportunities, a vision, and a plan to enhance global change and development through a networked environment. Another goal was to provide professional development, international projects, and programs to assist students in developing the skills and capacities for global success (Snyder et al., 2010, p. 7).

The Leadership Development Director felt compelled to provide GPP because of the overwhelming desire of the LSSD-trained school administrators to offer a memorable global experience for their students (Snyder et al., 2010). There have always been foreign exchange programs that are very good, but they sometimes seem to be only in schools where parents can afford them or efficiently fundraise the necessary money. Creating an experience that allowed everyone to participate on equal footing, no matter if the school had a higher or lower poverty level, was important. The idea was to do something memorable that everyone could afford.

Extensive planning determined which learning management system the District School Board of Pasco could provide for free to our schools and their global partners and would work in the United States, Sweden, and China. Finding video conferencing platforms that worked in the United States and Sweden was easy. Our partners in China worked very hard through trial and error to find one that worked for everyone (Snyder et al., 2010).

Pasco County provided technical support and hosted the orientation training. It was an extensive three-day training for Pasco County participants, with each school's principal, teacher(s), and technology specialist participating. The extreme organizational challenges became more manageable with an international oversight committee of at least one district coordinator from each participating school district. Their leadership and work were essential to the program's success, and the district coordinator then became responsible for organizing, training, and troubleshooting issues within their district's participating classes.

It was important that the asynchronous working environment was well organized and worked for all the schools; the initial program was comprised of 33 classes from schools in the three districts on three continents. One class from each district participated on one of the 11 teams. (Snyder et al., 2010) The other districts that joined Pasco were the Nanshan District in Shenzhen, China, and Stockholm City schools in Stockholm, Sweden.

Both training programs, MPS and LSSD, promoted the importance of reaching beyond the district, state, and national boundaries to form partnerships and learn with students and teachers overseas. Snyder et al. (2010) shared that there were two types of projects. The first was for classes to share about themselves, their school, and their community. This was very powerful. These were generally presented and recorded through the LMS. The second type involved a collaborative project carried out in all three classes across the three continents.

The teachers, parents, and administrators were elated watching the students' excitement and joy when they first connected through their video conferencing platform. Setting up the meeting across three time zones was challenging, but the Leadership Development Director will never forget one school that set up in the cafeteria and invited parents to attend. The children talked and laughed with their new friends as the parents beamed in the background. Because of their project work in a synchronous environment, it was as if they had always known one another.

It was inspiring to watch them talk about the similarities and differences between the water samples they collected and analyzed from the Baltic Sea, the Gulf of Mexico, and a river in Shenzhen (Snyder et al., 2010). The

KEYS TO REMEMBER

- Get the right people involved to make a complex program work.
- Respect differences, whether they are cultural, language, or time zones.
- Becoming more globally conscious is worth the effort for all stakeholders.
- Expect remarkable and unexpected results from the teachers' and students' efforts.

interviews reminded us of the many projects covering water conservation, recycling, folk music, and other topics.

In summary, many critical big ideas were evident through the implementation and impact of the GPP. All participants realized that even though each country has different traditions, languages, and cultures, the teachers and students were more alike than different. The students have the same issues, concerns, thoughts, and ideas about life regardless of their nationality. The hard organizational work was worth it, and ultimately all participants took positive steps toward becoming more knowledgeable and responsible global citizens.

A CALL TO ACTION

This twisting road of professional development for school administrators has continued to evolve for the Leadership Development Director. Leaving the school district and moving to the university, where he continues to coordinate a year-long principal certification program, has further opened his eyes to the power of a systems approach to leading.

MPS and LSSD training changed the course of a district and pushed it to a place of prominence within the state of Florida through the support of two superintendents. The overarching dedication to professional growth and excellence was supported by attention to systems thinking and quality management. The district was committed to the "why" of the training. Next, they connected the "how" to the "why" to make it actionable.

The Call to Action can start for everyone, no matter their situation. Consider the three big idea paragraphs and the Keys to Remember sections, which provide ideas that all leaders can use. Developing districtwide leadership is the most meaningful and powerful journey a district can take. Consistency of leadership and a commitment to an understood and shared vision starts with the superintendent. Engaging experts and being flexible throughout the process is necessary because positive and negative things will occur along the way.

There must be a connection to experts and finding practices supported by excellent research. Hard work toward a vision of excellence with the help of experts makes all the difference. An interview respondent noted that elementary, middle, high, technical, and all district services must work toward the same vision. Professional development must be provided to assist each area in working toward that vision.

MPS and LSSD were systems approaches and helped people to work together because all leaders must have ongoing training opportunities to strengthen systems thinking, as noted by interviewees. Interview respondents shared that MPS allowed people to feel involved and included through the commitment to collaboration. The staff input was valued, which developed a different level of respect. It strengthened my school because everyone could participate in the change and strengthened relationships.

Two significant impacts of MPS and LSSD are that the training is still highly relevant today because of the focus on systems and ideas transcending time, such as vision, positive change, collaboration, culture, and instructional excellence. Also, those trained mentored many aspiring leaders and included the ideas and concepts they learned in the other training. So, it will never grow old because the tools and study of systems will never be irrelevant. Dream big, work hard, and have fun.

REFERENCES

Burrello, L., Beitz, L., & Mann, J. (2016). *A Positive manifesto: How appreciative schools can transform public education.* Elephant Rock Books.

Cooperrider, D. L., & Whitney, D. (2005). *Appreciative inquiry: A positive revolution in change.* Berrett-Koehler Publishers, Inc.

Giella, M., & Stanfill, M. (1996). Concurrent school transformation: Resolving the dilemma. *NASSP Bulletin* 80, 58–66.

History Quotes. (2019). Alpha history. Retrieved August 20, 2022, from https://alphahistory.com/history-quotes/

Mann, J. L. (2023). Appreciative school systems: A path to school success. In K. J. Snyder & K. M. Snyder (Eds.), *Systems thinking for sustainable schooling: A mindshift for educators to lead and achieve quality schools.* Lanham, Md: Rowman and Littlefield.

Mann, J. L. (2022). Gulf Coast partnership program 2022 – 2023: Cohort 11—Session 2. PowerPoint.

Parkinson, A. (1990). An examination of reliability and factor structure of the school work culture profile (doctoral dissertation). The University of South Florida.

Scanga, D., & Sedlack, R. (2023). Networking for principal sustainability. In K. J. Snyder & K. M. Snyder (Eds.), *Systems thinking for sustainable schooling: A mindshift for educators to lead and achieve quality schools.* Lanham, MD: Rowman and Littlefield.

Snyder, K. J. (2023). Systems thinking and sustainable schooling: Foundations in physics. In K. J. Snyder & K. M. Snyder (Eds.), *Systems thinking for sustainable schooling: A mindshift for educators to lead and achieve quality schools.* Lanham, MD: Rowman and Littlefield.

Snyder, K. J. (2012). Welcome to LSSD training. *Leadership for sustainable school development principal training.* Training Manual. Pasco County School District. International School Connection, Inc.

Snyder, K. J., Mann, J. L., Johnson, E., & Zing, M. (2010). Schools without borders: The global partnership project of the ISC. *Innovation,* (Fall), 6–14.

Snyder, K. J., Acker-Hocevar, M., & Snyder, K. M. (2008). *Living on the edge of chaos: Leading schools into the global age.* ASQ: The Quality Press.

Snyder, K. J. (2008). Welcome to GPP training for school leaders. *Global partnership program principal, teacher, and technology specialist school training.* Training Manual. Pasco County School District. International School Connection, Inc.

Snyder, K. J. (2007). *Leading sustainable school development training: Capacities for leading sustainable development in educational institutions.* Training Manual. Pasco County School District. International School Connection, Inc.

Snyder, K. J., & Snyder, K. M. (1996). Developing integrated work cultures: Findings from a study on school change. *NASSP Bulletin*, 80 (576), 67–77.

Snyder, K. J. (1988). *Competency training for managing productive schools.* Harcourt Brace Jovanovich, Inc.

Snyder, K. J., & Anderson, R. H. (1986). *Managing productive schools: Toward an ecology.* Harcourt, Brace, and Jovanovich.

Chapter 5

Toward a Human Networked School

A Natural Energy System

Karolyn J. Snyder

Schooling as we know it today is in crisis mode, and static traditional practices are the culprit. Like all other organizations, schools have become so complex that the old rules of the game are no longer adequate, as the recent exodus of teachers and school leaders in the United States illustrates (Scanga & Sedlack, 2023; NASSP, 2022). Systems Thinking is required to reshape complex education systems for a sustainable future for both professionals and students. New structures for work, as well as new processes and systems of communication, are naturally emerging in the global community, where human networking is becoming a vital strategy.

A more dynamic energy system in schools will free the human spirit as educators work together toward preparing every student for a successful life in this rapidly changing world. Building connection systems that bind people together around a common purpose is a leadership opportunity, for collective energy is both personally satisfying and necessary for altering static approaches to schooling. Educators need a sustainable and dynamic work environment to promote responsive innovation and continuous improvement systems. A sustainable future of schooling depends on the transformation of schooling into a networking lifestyle.

The Head of Corbett Preparatory School at IDS, Nicholas Rodriguez, recently created a new hashtag that announces to the world that this pre-K through eighth-grade school functions as *#OneCommunity*. The purpose of this chapter is to share the natural evolution of Corbett Prep from a school with many isolated teams to a networked organization. This is a story of building a human energy system for growth that is based on systems thinking, which is both natural and available to all educators. In this chapter, the *Human Networked Organization* offers promise for reshaping schooling to fit the times.

Systems Thinking is central to shaping networked environments, with a focus on the continuous integration of forces and functions around a common purpose. Major shifts in thinking can evolve naturally, from bureaucratic hierarchies to holistic systems thinking, moving from parts to the whole with inherent multidisciplinarity, from objects to relationships, from measuring to mapping, from quantities to qualities, and from structures to processes (Capra & Luisi, 2016). These new habits of mind foster sustainable systems thinking that leads to networking and continuous adaptation.

The solution to living and working in increasingly complex organizations is to build a strong collective energy system. It is all about connections! Building a strong connection system creates the resiliency and responsiveness capacity to act "on a dime." A human networked organization, whether it's a school, school district, or state and federal agency, builds connection systems that naturally create the energy and elasticity to enable an organization to thrive in these complex times. Network thinking! Connection Systems! These are the energy-building pathways for sustainable living and working.

In part 1, the focus is on the rise of networking in organizational life everywhere. In part 2, networking science provides a foundation for creating a new mindset about schooling. The historical background of networking illustrates its importance to human activity since the dawn of civilization. Part 3 is a case study that features networking as a way of life for Corbett Preparatory School of IDS, an independent school that naturally evolved over time into a networked organization. In the final Call to Action, networking options are offered for educators to build a strong connection system around a student preparation agenda.

THE RISE OF HUMAN NETWORKING IN ORGANIZATIONAL LIFE

The global community is now so interconnected and complex that every feature of life is influenced by information, resources, challenges, and opportunities. This global dynamic has created a primal shift, with conflicting forces trying to either gain control over or create islands of development and sustainability. Mounting layers of complexity naturally forge a new kind of thinking in all work environments, whether it be in politics, finance, trade, agriculture, supply chains, or war.

It is time for educators to rise above the stranglehold of static traditions to function in step with the dynamic times that will transform the very foundations of schooling. Networks have become the new structures for the global age, and networking is fast becoming an essential leadership skill. Foundational for network living within and across organizations is a shift in our thinking, from compliance with static assumptions and practices to continuous adaptability to the rapidly changing features of living today.

Since the dawn of the human community, families have bonded together by connecting with each other around a common purpose. The creation of the bureaucratic movement by Max Weber (1922) was based on mechanical assumptions about the organization of people, which placed a stranglehold on adapting to changing conditions. Understanding how to build sustainable connection systems that are adaptive, responsive, and continuously improving naturally leads to networking within the organization, a practice that will foster both adaptability and sustainability.

Global networks have generated their own dynamic to attract knowledge, investment, and talent to form networks of technological innovation, and this new network environment raises questions about power and power relationships. Who are the owners? Who are the producers? Who are the managers? Who are the workers? Traditional features of work become increasingly blurred within the context of teamwork, networking, outsourcing, and subcontracting. In a networked environment, everyone possesses the power to help move the system forward (Acker-Hocevar, 2023).

This is a story about human energy and how it can be nurtured and unleashed in organizations to continually adapt to emerging challenges and opportunities. In a PBS Series on television, Niall Ferguson (2020) put forth the idea that networks are now the dominant form of communication in the world, replacing centralized communications through organizational hierarchies.

NETWORKING SCIENCE

While networking has been the natural human connection process since the dawn of civilization (Kramer, 1963), networking theory and science emerged as late as the 1960s around the concept of six degrees of separation between people in Random Networks (Watts, 2003). The Scale-Free Network was born in the 1990s after scholars studied the ways large computer networks and human networks emerge (Barabasi, 2016); scale-free networks are dominated by hubs of activity that stimulate a network's growth.

Early theories featured networks as static structures, but more recent research (Watts, 2003) documents that networks are a dynamic phenomenon because they evolve and change over time and are driven by the activities or decisions of those very components. Digital communication technology has not only driven global innovation and productivity; it also enables people everywhere to engage in social networking at a rapid rate.

In this connected age, what happens and how it happens depends on a network's health (Watts, 2003). This finding suggests that energy and synchrony matter to a network's growth, for energy is generated by the members and their connections. A network simply defined: "is nothing more than a collection of objects (or people) connected to each other in some fashion" (Watts, 2003). A network can only be understood as a whole, and the function of emerging parts to the whole (Buchanan, 2002). Scientists have learned that a network grows from within itself, rather than from external forces, as it responds continuously to changing conditions and opportunities (Barabasi, 2003). The Science of Complexity now searches for patterns in networks that make them vital and sustainable. Scientists are examining networks as the new structures for the global age, where networking is fast becoming a primary leadership skill.

According to Barabasi (2003), the 21st century is likely to concentrate on Complexity and the Network, which he predicts will have the following characteristics:

- A network is a rapidly evolving dynamic system of interconnectedness.
- The Scale-Free Network idea is built around Hubs of interest.
- Networks are self-organizing and based on the strength of Hubs.
- Hubs have many internal nodes and links.
- Hubs connect to other Hubs through weak links, thus forming the network.
- Large Hubs define the direction and shape of the network.
- Two laws govern networks: growth and preferential attachment.

If the network pattern for work is now a dominant feature in 21st-century life, what are the implications for management and for network development in institutions of all kinds? Barabasi (2003) argues that the -twenty-first-century Business Model will move from hierarchy to networks in the following ways.

- Organizations will shed hierarchical thinking and develop networking thinking.
- Network hubs get bigger and stronger as they connect with each other.
- A network is governed by the biggest hubs, which keep the network together.
- Strategic partnerships and alliances are the means of survival for networks.
- Each Hub must add value to the network for it to become sustainable.

The opportunity for leaders is to create processes that build energy through connections that sustain continuous improvement and innovation. The idea of energy being generated through connection systems is grounded in the laws of Quantum Physics and Systems Thinking, along with Chaos and Complexity theories (Snyder, 2023). Consider these six laws from physics:

- Connections promote the growth and development of living systems.
- Disequilibrium stimulates transformative adaptations to new conditions.
- Natural Systems evolve from feedback within and outside the system.
- Complex adaptive systems respond to and act as a system of influence.
- Information is a driver of change in a system, for it provides direction.
- Human intention is a driver for improving the quality of life for everyone.

Continuous adaptation to changing conditions is the primary challenge for schooling today, and more energy is needed now for both extra and different tasks on the journey forward. How might the power of connections be strengthened? Einstein changed the way we think about how the universe works, shifting from static and fixed assumptions to those grounded in the idea that the universe is continuously changing (Isaacson, 2009). The universe is a dynamic living system. It is time for educators to abandon the idea of "fixed anything" and operate under the assumption that the school is also a living system, which needs to be continuously nurtured.

Einstein invented a "spooky communication system at a distance," which expands our notions of energy formulation and its power. Einstein called this phenomenon "Entanglement," which is based on atomic energy (Clegg, 2006). When the heat from electrons in an atom is sufficiently strong, certain particles become extremely excited and are propelled into fast action forming a connection that endures over time and space. Quantum entanglement has become one of the central principles of quantum physics today, although not yet fully understood (Jones, 2017).

The power of entanglement can be observed in schools that perpetuate both personal and professional connections, which become enduring over time and space. A current PhD student at Mid Sweden University is studying what she calls the "Sticking Power" of Corbett Prep (Rouse, 2022). She is exploring why so many former graduates, parents, grandparents, teachers, and other workers stay connected or come back to contribute to this school's continuous journey. The power of entanglement!

NETWORKING AS A WAY OF LIFE AT CORBETT PREP

A basic idea for building a school's energy system is fostering strong connections within and across work units. This current age of connections is built upon teams, coalitions, networks, and partnerships for learning, exploring, and living on the edge of chaos (Snyder et al., 2000, 2008). The energy within organizations emerges naturally from interconnected healthy, growing networks of human activity around a unifying purpose, as well as from continuous feedback with new ideas and resources that promote continuous development.

It recently became apparent that Corbett Prep had evolved into a structure that was no longer familiar. As a researcher, curiosity about this phenomenon led to a closer exploration of the school's current structure and communication system. It appears that over time, teaming, which is the founding organizational structure of the school, began connecting with each other naturally. Eventually, a few teachers were also trained in a new specialty for the entire school. Over the years, Corbett Prep evolved naturally into a networked system where everything is interconnected with clearly defined hubs, clusters, and links between hubs and clusters. A new kind of continuous energy became apparent for addressing a growing complexity at all levels.

Corbett Preparatory School at IDS is an independent school in Tampa, Florida, in the United States with about 570 students, pre-K through middle school, and which recently celebrated its 50th anniversary. (Cohen, 2003). Joyce B. Swarzman led the school's growth and development for over 25 years, promoting development and connections across the school that led to a network way of life. Nicholas Rodriguez, the current head of the school, continues to build this dynamic networked system with his unique perspectives that are unleashing new levels of talent and energy among all workers.

Students at the school are organized into teams or learning communities with teachers who work with three or four other specialists, aides, and student teachers. Given the apparent teacher shortage today, a team structure of many students with adults who possess differing levels of teaching qualifications holds great promise. Teams are the essential building block for a human-networked school organization that is natural and self-generating.

Professional staff members at Corbett Prep participate in weekly workshops, while small groups and individuals also engage in a variety of additional programs to advance their own knowledge and then to strengthen the school's performance. State, national, and international student, staff, and team awards are common, as is the recognition of the school as outstanding. Four members of the administration and faculty are also enrolled in a PhD program at Mid Sweden University, researching features of Corbett Prep and its successes from a Quality Management perspective. What are the forces that are propelling this school forward?

For over 25 years, the school's development journey has been grounded in Systems Thinking (Snyder et al., 2000), Quality Management (Deming, 2000; Juran, 1989; Snyder et al., 2000), and Chaos Theory (Snyder et al., 2000, 2008), which serve as guideposts to support organizational sustainability, continuous improvement, and customer satisfaction (https://www.corbettprep.com). The school's student population has increased recently, as have the continuous awards for outstanding performance in Florida, throughout the United States, and on the global stage.

In this purpose-driven, student success organization, workers naturally take on new chores and challenges in response to the emerging demands of a living, growing system. The phenomenon is clearly a network of growing clusters of initiatives, with new kinds of leadership roles emerging, and where human energy is a force for innovation. Corbett Prep's network didn't happen overnight because of administrative directives but rather emerged naturally over the decades as the professional staff and school leaders pursued ideas for continuously enriching the learning environment for its students.

Over time, school leaders shifted their work from supervising individuals, teams, and programs to managing the systems of work throughout the school's network, along with the health of the school's culture and its impact on every learner. Teachers are responsible for everything that occurs within their learning communities while mentoring and coaching each other to "Olympic" performance. Many teachers take on additional major responsibilities for the entire school, which strengthens the school's connection system, its purpose and values, and its sustainability potential.

The administrative team appears to have one purpose, which is to support the work of teachers in achieving high success levels for all students. What now exists is a complex web of life with its energy for learning, where every student is cherished and nurtured, a phenomenon which is apparent to every student and parent, as well as to the hundreds of national and international visitors to the school each (normal) year.

A complex web of life proved essential for the success of Corbet Prep to continue delivering quality education throughout the pandemic. In a study of their Hybrid Model (Snyder et al., 2021) it was evident that teaching and interconnected systems of work became the driver that enabled the school to develop and deliver a new model of schooling that is based on hybrid learning. Data from the "well-being" study conducted by the Contentment Foundation demonstrated that the school not only survived; it thrived. Teachers and school leaders attribute this success to the network model of living at Corbett Prep.

Corbett Prep is an example of a natural networked system. Three network features provide the enduring structure for continuous adaptation and innovation: 1) Hubs of work, 2) Clusters of work, and 3) Links that promote interconnectivity and work of the network.

HUBS: Hubs are the most highly connected features of the network. In a *Human Networked School*, academic learning communities are the hubs, which are the primary and strongest energy force in the school. At Corbett Prep, a strong system of values is found in 20 core programs that support learning and the curriculum and bind the hubs together with common valued practices.

CLUSTERS: Work in the smaller units is purpose oriented while related and connected to the Hubs and to the primary purpose of the organization. In a *Human Networked School*, Clusters are those special programs, activities, and events that enhance learning opportunities for all students and are connected to each Hub. In many cases, Clusters also connect with each other to support events.

LINKS: It is because of Links that a network forms and grows. Links make the difference between silos of connected work and a network of interconnected work. The Links connect Clusters to each other and to the Hubs. Links in a *Human Networked School* are the many teacher leaders who assume additional responsibilities for the whole school, who become experts in something important, and who are connected to all Clusters and academic Hubs.

The interconnectivity of hubs and clusters, through links, is vital for developing a complex, cohesive, and strong network for sustainable growth. An important law of physics about the continuous health of a network is that negative energy grows negatively, while positive energy grows positively (Snyder et al., 2008). To keep the network's pathways open, positive energy is pursued, while negative energy is stopped. A network grows when the communication channels are open between and among programs and services, and where there is clarity of purpose (student success) that drives the learning and work for everyone.

ACADEMIC HUBS

The first unit of analysis to consider is Corbett Prep's Hubs of work, which are the dominant units in a network. In Figure 5.1, the five academic Hubs are the major work units for every teacher and all other academic professionals. Their primary purpose is "developing the whole child." Students are organized into both multiaged and age-specific teams, which generates a fluid system for academic purposes school-wide.

NETWORK HUBS
Primary teaching responsibilities and academics

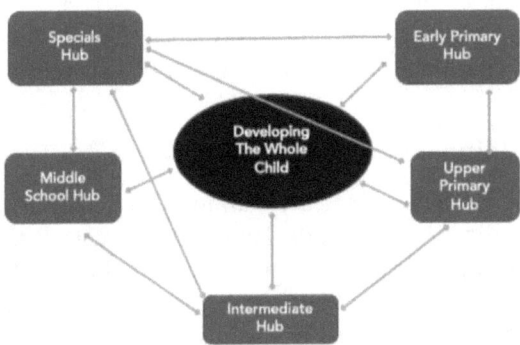

Figure 5.1. Corbett Prep's Network of Hubs

Core Values

Corbett Prep is guided by a strong set of core values that are grounded in pedagogical philosophy and theories of human development, social relations, leadership, and global citizenry. These values have developed over time and form the school's central guiding document: The M.O.R.E. Approach (More Options for Results in Education) (Cohen, 2003). These core learning systems, featured in Figure 5.2, are vital to the continuous cohesiveness of the school's values, culture, and network development.

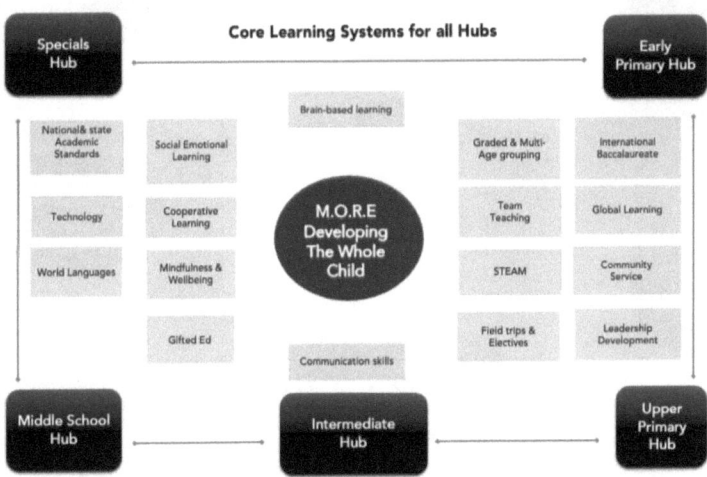

Figure 5.2. Core Values Embedded in the M.O.R.E.

For example, all Hubs (Early Childhood, Middle School, etc.) integrate core values, mindfulness, team teaching, global learning, social-emotional learning, cooperative learning, etc., into their pedagogical praxis and curricula. While the academic content differs for each age-grade level, the core values are present at all levels. As well, the staff serves as role models for students in their behaviors, attitudes, and language to reflect the values, while students in turn coach one another based on the shared values.

Clusters of Additional Programs and Services

Surrounding the academic Hubs are learning Clusters, illustrated in Figure 5.3, which are utilized by each of the Hubs to support academic development with programs that further advance student growth. Five of the Clusters provide enrichment programs for learning and social development (arts, music and drama, technology, physical education, and international experiences), while three Clusters (technology, administration, and Board of Trustees) provide the support system for the school to function as a living system.

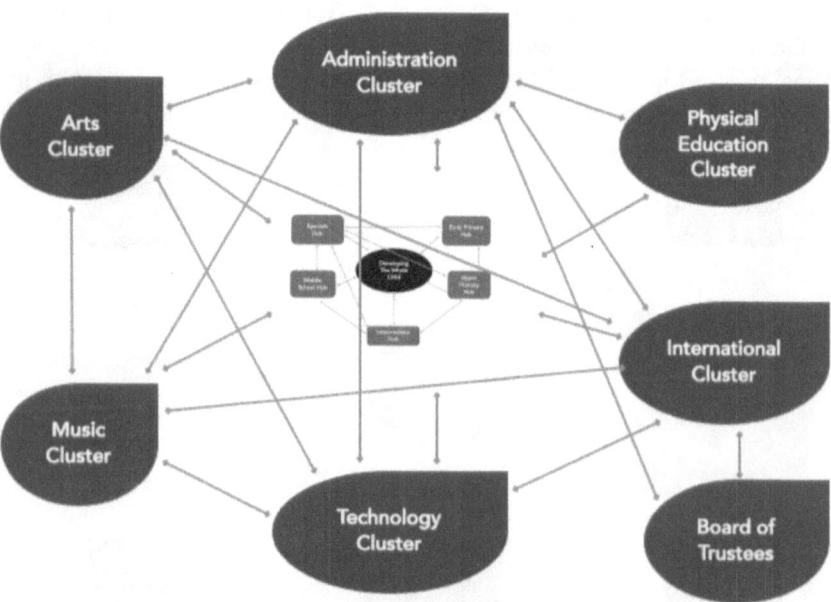

Figure 5.3. Corbett Prep's Clusters of Program and Services

The arrows illustrate actual working relationships between and among Hubs and Clusters. For example, the Arts cluster is also connected to the Music and Drama cluster and to the Technology cluster for school-wide performances, reflecting an interdependent approach to the arts and technology for learning. The Administration cluster is connected to all clusters as a central support system, while the Trustees provide overall guidance for the continuous development of the school as a healthy living system. Gone is isolation in any form at Corbett Prep, for networking (as in #OneCommunity) is the driver.

NETWORK LINKS

Figure 5.4 illustrates the kinds of programs and connections that exist within the work of the school's different clusters connecting them with hubs. The network model is apparent with its many school-wide events that take place throughout the school year. For example, during Grandparents Day, which is offered once a year, everyone participates in a school-wide performance, which is developed and orchestrated by teachers from the Music and Drama. Art, and Technology clusters, and involves students from all academic hubs. The network links distinguish a networked school from other schools, where Hubs may or may not be connected to each other, and the Clusters of non-academic work may or may not be connected to each other and/or to the

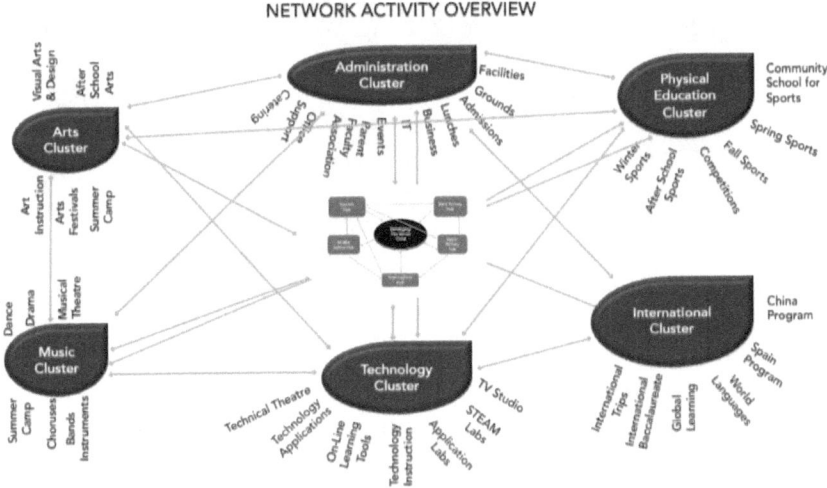

Figure 5.4. The Human Network of Activity at Corbett Preparatory School

academic hubs. Links in the network create the connection system that distributes vital information, knowledge, resources, and feedback, enabling the network to stay open and expand over time.

In the Corbett Prep story, links are the secondary responsibilities of selected teachers. The arrows reflect actual functional links for school-wide responsibilities. Selected teachers are sent for special training in their area of school leadership to provide overall training, guidance, supervision, and accountability for the success of their program school-wide.

The 18 network Links in Figure 5.5 identify existing school-wide programs at Corbett Prep that function under the leadership of one or several teachers. Links are responsible for gaining knowledge about the new initiative, teaching everyone else the basics, and then ensuring the success of the programs. The work that emerges from the Links adds complex requirements to each academic Hub. The response is continuous integration and adaptation while maintaining what is working and tossing out that which has become outdated or irrelevant.

Recently, additional links have been added for working with the entire school, with existing professional staff playing leadership roles: a *Wellness link* and a *Student Success* link. A New Application Lab promotes the use of Legos, Stem projects, and other digital approaches to learning and development, and the network links continue to grow.

This dance of complex adaptation is now the norm for Corbett Prep's entire professional and administrative Hubs and Clusters, which function within a culture of continuous improvement and clarity about purpose and values. The *Human Networked Organization*, as a prototype, shows great promise for unleashing human energy to create new pathways for work and for sustainable outcomes in this complex age of living. Within the networked organization, growth self generates around common values, which leads to new levels of productivity and innovation.

NETWORK LINKS

• Curriculum Studies	• Division/School Leaders
• International Baccalaureate	• Yale's 4 Pillars of well-being
• Kagen Cooperative Learning	• ISC School Partnerships
• ISC Global Learning Integration	• Math School Wide
• Division Musicals	• Fine Arts Festivals
• Whole School Musicals	• Community School of the Arts
• STEAM Program & Exhibitions	• Language Arts School Wide
• Community School of Sports	• Modeling Teaching for Visitors

Figure 5.5. The 16 Network Links at Corbett Preparatory School

A CALL TO ACTION

In a recent interview with Dr. David Scanga, who recently retired from many years as assistant superintendent of schools in Pasco County Florida, shared ideas that foster the natural and sustainable development of networking within public schools. These are natural human activities, which are within reach of all schools and school districts:

- Organize all workers into multitalented teams, with varying levels of credentialing.
- Foster connections between and among teams to enrich learning.
- Promote adaptations to changing conditions.
- Expect innovation for the improvement of practice.
- Build the school's culture around a shared purpose and common values.
- Insist on a positive, forward-looking culture of work.
- Let go of power and instead empower teams with accountability.
- Shift the primary focus to building a growing energy system for student success.
- Continuously study a school's student data to identify how to strengthen the networking system.
- Build in time for people to network during the school day; this is essential!

For school district leaders, there are many opportunities to promote networking within schools. First, link principals together to learn with and from each other about the power and value of, and the strategies for, networking. Provide training for school leaders and district leaders in the concepts and the skills of networking, which stimulates a mind-shift to Systems Thinking and Quality Management for school development.

Central to the network's sustainability is the continual free flow of information with opportunities to pursue and invent new connected programs and services. These conditions energize everyone to connect, learn, and excel, which is a self-generating force. Let us embrace Human Network Thinking for sustainable development, which can open new pathways of opportunity and innovation to advance not only the education enterprise worldwide but also all human organizations that add value to the human community and its sustainability.

Let's transform the energy system of schools for the sustainability of schooling as a social enterprise! The *Human Networked Organization* provides a sustainable pathway forward!

REFERENCES

Acker-Hocevar, M. (2023). A Quantum worldview of responsive power for sustainable learning. In K. J. Snyder & K. M. Snyder (Eds.), *Systems thinking for sustainable schooling: A mindshift for educators to lead and achieve quality in schools.* Lanham, MD: Rowman and Littlefield Publishers.

Barabasi, A. (2016). *Network science.* Cambridge: Cambridge University Press.

Barabasi, A. (2003). *Linked: How everything is connected to everything else and what it means for business, science, and everyday life.* Auckland, New Zealand: PLUME, published by the Penguin Group.

Buchanan, M. (2002). *NEXUS: small worlds and the groundbreaking theory of networks.* New York: W. W. Norton & Company.

Capra, F., & Luisi, P. L. (2016). *The systems view of life: A unifying vision.* Cambridge University Press.

Cohen, D., and the Faculty and Staff of Corbett Preparatory School at IDS. (2003). *It's all about kids: every child deserves a "teacher of the year."* Bee Happy Publishing.

Clegg, B. (2006). *The god effect: Quantum entanglement, science's strangest phenomenon.* St. Martin's Griffin.

Deming, W. E. (2000). *Out of crisis,* Cambridge, MA: MIT Press.

Ferguson, N. (2020). *Niall Ferguson's Networld.* A three-part film documentary. https://www.pbs.org/wnet/networld/niall-fergusons-network-about/

Isaacson, W. (2018). *Einstein: the man. the genius, and the theory of relativity.* Andre Deutsch.

Juran, J. M. (1989). *Juran on leadership for quality: An executive handbook.* New York: The Free Press, a Division of Macmillan, Inc.

Kramer, S. (1963). *The Sumerians: Their history, culture and character.* Chicago: University of Chicago Press.

Rouse, K. S. (2022). "Sticking power": Finding quality in organizational culture and employee wellbeing influencing an intention to stay. Research paper presented at the 9th International Conference on Mechanics and Materials in Design, Madeira, Portugal.

Scanga, D., & Sedlack, R. (2023). Networking for principal sustainability. In K. J. Snyder & K. M. Snyder (Eds.), *Systems thinking for sustainable schooling: A mindshift for educators to lead and achieve quality in schools.* Lanham, MD: Rowman and Littlefield Publishers.

Snyder, K. M., Johnson, M., & Snyder, K. J. (2021). Going hybrid on a dime: Lessons from schooling during the pandemic and implications for sustainable quality in education. Paper presented at the 14th Annual International Conference on Education: Research and Innovation, Madrid, November 8–10, 2021.

Snyder, K. M, Ingelsson, P., & Bäckström, I. (2018). Using design thinking to support value-based leadership for sustainable quality development. *Business Process Management Journal,* 24(6), 1289–1301.

Snyder, K. J. (2023). Systems thinking and sustainable schooling: Foundations in physics. In K. J. Snyder & K. M. Snyder (Eds.), *Systems thinking for sustainable schooling: A mindshift for educators to lead and achieve quality in schools.* Lanham, MD: Rowman and Littlefield Publishers.

Snyder, K. J., Acker-Hocevar, M., & Snyder, K. M. (2000, 2008). *Living on the edge of chaos: leading schools into the global age.* Milwaukee: ASQ, The Quality Press

Watts, D. J. (2003). *Six degrees: The science of a connected age.* New York: W. W. Norton & Company, Inc.

Weber, Max. (1922). Bureaucracy. In H. Gerth & C. W. Mills (Eds.), *Max Weber: Essays in sociology.* Oxford University Press.

Zimmerman Jones, A. (2017). Quantum entanglement in physics: What it means when two particles are entangled. ThoughtCo (July 10). https://www.thoughtco.com/what-is-quantum-entanglement-2699355

Chapter 6

The Magic of Esprit de Corps Isn't Really Magic

John Fitzgerald, PhD

> *The basic principles of Systems Thinking (integration of everything around a common purpose) and Chaos Theory (change evolves in complex and unpredictable patterns) were combined for this continuing journey of school development with a Systems Thinking mindset.* (Snyder, 2023: p. 9)

The very survival of the human community today depends on how we think about progress, success, and change. Living and working have become so complex that they can only be understood systemically; *everything is interconnected and interdependent* (Martensson & Snyder, 2023). Sustainability has emerged over recent decades as a promising mindset and way of living in which the human community continues its forward development.

Sustainability is defined here as the growth of a living system as it responds to changing conditions. Creating sustainable conditions for learning requires a departure from isolation, which is a fundamental shift toward *systems thinking*. Pursuing the values of *Sustainability* will ensure an equitable and meaningful school system, which will require us to adopt *systems thinking* as a way of life (Snyder & Anderson, 1986).

This unique story is a critical read for school leaders who are overrun with school-related problems and seek sensible solutions to operating a complicated school. This story is a microcosm of the global reality of sustainability and concerns the daily problems and issues which can occur in any school. It is the narrative of a *turnaround school*, one which was down and rediscovered its potential through a *systems thinking* approach to organization. This is an important and practical story for educators as an accounting of the path of a successful cultural rebuild that resulted in a positive, stable, and safe learning environment.

The purpose of this chapter is to demonstrate how through purposeful and shared decision-making, using a systems approach to school organization, a school survived and eventually thrived over time. A like-minded leadership team believed that when addressing organizational issues, one needed to consider the whole school as a complete system and seek solutions complementing every part of the school. The approach initially involved building trust and support among all stakeholders, then developing cooperative endeavors across all sections and interest groups, and eventually supporting all levels through networked collaborations.

Part 1 of the chapter lends background information first from the coaching and sports world and then from the physics described by Snyder's (2022) natural energy model; Part 2 describes first two years and the difficult beginnings toward a culture change; Part 3 narrates events crucial to the overall success and a maturing of the school's culture; Part 4 recounts how the school completed a curriculum *case study review*, which reaffirmed the turnaround; and Part 5 is a Synthesis of that turnaround and a Call to Action.

BACKGROUND

In this chapter, we explore the development of positive energy that emerges among individuals and groups when a networked organization operates with interdependent people developing ideas and alternatives in a creative and supportive milieu.

A Lesson from Coaching and Sports

Leaders, coaches, and successful teachers see a systems development process as an important and necessary environmental approach to building an effective and focused team. Organizational success is the result of working collaboratively as a group toward a set of clear goals and aspirations and is based upon positive interrelationships built by human networks within the organization.

Mark Messier (2021), in his book *No One Wins Alone: A Memoir*, said, "If you want to go somewhere fast, go by yourself. If you want to go far, go together (p. 87)," All participants must be on the same page, with the same clear goal(s), where every single participant knows her role and is valued for it. Messier adds, "It's critical for leaders to create an environment where colleagues have a collective purpose. . . . People are inspired by organizations that have a shared vision. . . . They take pride in their work, and a culture of trust and commitment is created" (p. 47).

Effective leaders and coaches have known the magic of *esprit de corps* (team spirit) for years. Training programs, such as those created by Performance Learning Systems (PLS), have incorporated key elements to support a how-to approach to developing team spirit. PLS, in its seminal training course Project T.E.A.C.H. (Hasenstab, 1989), outlined the process this way:

1. People join organizations (clubs, teams, schools) together because they have a common interest or a common goal;
2. To feel part of the organization, every individual wants or needs to contribute to the whole group's goal or direction. If that individual does not feel that they can contribute, they leave the group of their own accord;
3. Every member of the group demonstrates appreciation for every other member's contribution(s) or role. If any member feels unappreciated for their contribution, they leave the group (physically or mentally);
4. Given the above, there becomes a genuine *collective appreciation* of each member's contribution. This is the "Esprit de Corps" or "team spirit that is represented by behavioral and motivational *energy* that puts each member on a common mission.

Successful teams find harmony and balance. It is a matter of everyone playing their part by bringing her energy to the circle . . . and it doesn't happen overnight. (Messier, p. 147)

A Lesson from Physics

A natural phenomenon described by Snyder et al. (2008, 2023) indicates that when people are encouraged and appreciated in their role in an organization and are working in a way meaningful to themselves and the whole group, there is a positive energy generated that serves to support and motivate that group. The emphasis is on not just how they fit together but on how they relate (Snyder et al., 2008). In this case, that might mean, how they *rub each other the right way* to create energy.

This replicates Snyder's (2023) energy model in which electrons from different atoms "rub together" to create actual positive physical energy. When that energy is directed toward the work goal, the evolving solution or product becomes a self-motivating task. The culture of that organizational team is transformed into an enhanced way of doing things.

Consider the following three elements summarized in this description of the physics analogy from Snyder et al. (2008, pp. 62–63).

- *Element 1: Disequilibrium Leads to Self-Organization*: A state of disequilibrium holds a self-renewal and self-organizational function. An organization's goal is to establish equilibrium, but disequilibrium is the state in which any system is the most spontaneous, adaptive, and creative, and can prompt new kinds of collective action.
- *Element 2: Positive Connections Lead to Interconnectivity and Networking*: If there are no connections in an organization, there is no energy for growth. Where there are organization-wide work teams and networks, an organization will generate its energy system. Connections are central to energy creation and sustainable change.
- *Element 3: Complexity Leads to Complex Adaptive Systems:* Living systems are never in equilibrium because they are inherently unstable and therefore complex. However, complexity is a natural feature of thriving systems, which grow in unpredictable ways.

The International School Connection (ISC) *Model of Sustainable Schooling* (Fitzgerald & Sullivan, 2023) maintains that all systems in the school work to support educators as they nurture and develop student capacity for sustainable living and learning. The three elements above have been adapted to the ISC model to support schools. Disequilibrium is a natural indicator of where attention and direction are needed to strengthen an area of school organization, and this is accomplished by establishing connections and thus energy into the existing networks. The following illustrates how this might be accomplished following disequilibrium.

THE BEGINNINGS OF CULTURE CHANGE

Surprise: Day One Disequilibrium

No one told the principal until the week before the fall term began. The superintendent called on Monday just before the news broke. One of the male staff at the school had been arrested and accused of abusing two Grade 8 girls just before school closed for the summer. The vice-principal and the principal (both new to the school) decided that their first priority was the well-being and the safe environment of the whole school of teachers and staff, and the community of children and parents they served.

As children returned to school on the first day, the principal warded off the press while at the same time welcoming busses, students who walked to school, and their parents. The principal stationed himself at the bus drop-off right in front of the school, and the vice-principal placed herself at the other bus entrance. For the next four years, the principal and vice-principal team were in those positions every morning to welcome everyone and every afternoon when they went home. The effect of that consistent presence was a powerful signal for students and parents!

The intent to keep everyone in the building safe, secure, and ready to learn was essential. Within the first two weeks of the semester, the school council (a parent advisory group required of all provincial schools) met with the leadership team. They were concerned about the situation, the well-being of their children, and the image of the school and the community. After four months, the charges were dropped for "lack of evidence." The girls, now in Grade 9, had fabricated their story to retaliate for a low grade on an assignment. The teacher returned to his assignment, to his team, and to his students.

Over the course of that term, the administrative team had slowly begun to gain the trust of the teachers and parents of the community. In the face of this "disequilibrium," the staff and the community fought hard to follow normal routines. The trust gained was the first step of a four-year team-building and networking process. Mann (2023) emphasizes that engendering trust and capacity building among team members involves investing oneself with a genuine interest in others' lives. The importance of being visible, and available, building respect, modeling positivity, and caring supports the development of a positive, supportive, and loyal culture.

The Library Room Issue: Disequilibrium and the First Decision

The library was a large room and had great potential as a meeting area. The disequilibrium came from the teachers who saw the computer lab installed in the library as a distraction. At the end of the first month, a reorganization of classes and teaching responsibilities had to be completed due to a change in the school population, and reorganization is always a disruption.

With the drop in student numbers, a classroom became available. The room was close to the center of the school, and it would be easy to rewire. After conferring with division heads and other teacher leaders, the decision was made to move the computer lab into the available room. This was a popular move for the school and the faculty. The initial disequilibrium led to the need for a creative and collaborative solution in response to many of the teachers' expressed need for change.

The consultation process among three divisions demonstrated the first collaborative decision and the new leadership and showed that the school could be successful amidst the turmoil of that first semester. This *responsive power* fuels creative answers as co-participants work together to solve problems (Acker-Hocevar, Cruz-Janzen, & Wilson, 2012). Martensson & Snyder (2023) suggest that when there is a significant link between leadership and staff involvement, employees feel they have the opportunity to influence decision-making, thereby minimizing future resistance.

Team Building, Task One: Belief Statement

Toward the end of the first term, the principal clarified what was expected of the school by the school district over the next year. Each school was required to establish a Mission/Vision Statement. In the eyes of the teaching staff, this represented significant "disequilibrium" because, traditionally, these statements were created but never followed up on in any meaningful way. This traditional inconsistency created "a waste of time" disequilibrium for the faculty and staff.

Initially, at a general staff meeting, the principal asked everyone to sit in groups mixing a variety of division teachers and other staff personnel. The principal explained the collaborative process for this work and assured that it would take only the one hour allocated for that meeting and no more than two more hours of regular staff meeting time. He held to that timing promise.

First, he asked each person to write one sentence: What did they believe to be important about what we do in this school? Next, he asked people to pair up, share, and combine what they had written. Then he asked for groups of four, then eight, to complete the same process, and they in turn developed a written statement. After sharing, many noted how similar the initial statements appeared to be. A volunteer from each group of 16 joined a "wordsmith group" that would choose the wording for a common statement.

At the next meeting, after discussing the common statement, the principal asked each person to write one sentence, "How would they need to work to achieve what they believed?" With different partners and groups, the same process ensued. When these efforts were completed, a different set of volunteers was asked to bring the second part of the process together with the first. At a third meeting, the combined statement was reviewed. The staff had collaboratively designed a two-sentence belief statement that was to serve as a *draft* Mission-Vision Statement for the next four years. This belief statement was reviewed annually by all.

Virtually everyone involved had played some type of role in its creation. When a controversial issue appeared, the school went to the belief statement to check collective values. For many, having a recognized role in the exercise was instrumental to giving value to both people and processes and strengthening staff commitment to the school. Mann (2023) indicates that to align major systems and subsystems, groups must collaboratively establish clear values and a core purpose that can become a guide to support future work and decisions.

Team Building, Task Two: Curriculum Implementation

The principal, aware of the provincial curriculum implementation task which lay ahead, emphasized the importance of the work and the hope of involving as many teachers as possible. The principal indicated that the school would work on two documents in each school year for the next three or four years. The first two documents selected would be Math and Science & Technology. He insisted that there would be no pressure or rush to complete the process. Committee members were interested in volunteers from each division.

The principal would guide the process with groups of up to eight people. Meetings would take place in February and early March, with a total of four or five two-hour meetings for each group, and dinner would be provided after each meeting.

The first meeting established the document's "Big Ideas" and a plan about how it could be introduced to the staff during several training sessions. The committee would be responsible for training the rest of the staff. As this plan developed over the five meetings, teachers were surprised with their progress and their commitment to each of the two projects. After the initial meetings, the committees continued to meet regularly to review their progress to date and recommend changes. "It is the leader's job to set benchmarks and sell the vision. The leader then assures people 'we can do this,' and 'this is how'" (Messier, 2021: p. 48).

When each team took their plans to the faculty, their energy inspired colleagues. As each team had members from across divisions and speciality areas, those members appealed to their peers, and ownership spread from each committee. Leaders use a living system's natural behavioral processes such as networking and self-organizing to produce information and meaning to respond effectively and proactively to the environment. A systems-thinking leader distributes power by influencing a critical mass of participants to develop new thinking patterns about accessing, constructing, and using knowledge (Sullivan, 2023).

The complexity of these committees created a strong bond among teachers at every level. Empowering people helps to build a culture of commitment and ownership. The purposeful language of systems-thinking leaders builds community and develops a common language and a shared history that creates the energy and knowledge for thinking positively to support change (Sullivan, 2023). The next year, and for the ensuing years, these committees met regularly to plan school-wide workshops and review each division's progress and address areas of concern.

Social Studies and The Arts Curricula Implementation: The next year, the principal called for volunteers to form two more committees, one for Social Studies and one for The Arts. These two groups were to work as before, to create plans to implement these curricula. Thirty-two teachers were now involved with their "favorite subjects" using a common language in the implementation activity. Curriculum work was becoming an energizing school activity! These groups learned how to implement curriculum through collegial discussion and planning, and each group became stronger and more confident with the process. They developed their energy.

The goal and possibility is the natural synthesis of ideas that occurs when individuals are free to engage in dialogue and collaborate on meaningful approaches to problems (Acker–Hocevar, 2023). The leadership was informally asking each group to become leaders for their divisions in this curriculum endeavor. The leadership used the school's positive core, all its people, to influence and inspire staff to willingly take action for the growth of the organization.

The Physical and Health Education and Kindergarten-Primary Curriculum Implementation: This process took place in the third year. The school embarked on a similar plan for these documents, and the teachers were quite confident as to how they would approach the task. The system's purpose for this ongoing work was to illustrate to everyone that the curriculum needed to be managed and supported as a sustainable professional activity completed by the teachers themselves. The school now had over 50 teachers involved in the curriculum integration process, all of them volunteers through division level or subject interest.

ON THE ROAD TO CULTURE CHANGE, TWO BIG ISSUES

Food Allergy Procedure: The Disequilibrium of Life and Death

Pressure had been mounting from the school district community for a set of guidelines for children with food allergies. A number of students at the school had food allergies, and all teachers were regularly informed as to that "deadly" reality. The vice-principal led a work group made up of interested community parents, teachers, and caretaking staff to devise school procedures that would help protect children with food allergies.

Near the end of that year, this group published thorough guidelines intended to protect children when eating lunch and snacks at school as well as to specify the cleaning procedures after each. The guidelines were presented to the School Council and then sent on to the general school community as a newsletter asking for parents' input and suggestions. Of the families of the approximately 750 students at the school, seven took issue with some of the guidelines. These parents were contacted, and the issues were discussed and details explained and agreed upon before the summer vacation.

This committee work represented a serious collaboration by all school community members. All but the parent members had union affiliates that dealt with the possible extra workload for members, and the important networking that crossed labor boundaries bodes well for future issues. The vice-principal helped the group to understand what was expected and allowed each person to find their motivation for the task (Messier, 2021: p. 48).

The next part of the food allergy story, however, brought a dangerous disequilibrium to the table. The week before the school opened at the start of the next school year, the principal read an article in the local newspaper entitled "The FB School Bans Peanuts." Two families had taken exception to the food allergy guidelines but had failed to take advantage of the feedback opportunity offered the previous spring. Late in the summer, they went to the media with their objections, saying their rights were being violated.

After consulting with the school staff, school council, and the superintendent, the principal called a series of meetings seeking to air the disagreements. The meetings were scheduled twice a month, with an agenda that would give voice to both sides of the controversy. Ground rules were set for these meetings, one of which was to stop any meetings that got emotionally out of hand and reconvene them the following week. The biweekly meetings would last until the issue was settled to the satisfaction of both groups.

Ultimately, the issue was resolved. The guideline required three wording changes and one physical adjustment to the original plan. The lesson conveyed to the whole school community was that the school, anchored by its values and beliefs, was willing to solve difficult problems appropriately.

Province-Wide Testing: A Mandate

The province-wide tests for Grades 3 and 6 were designed to measure the progress of schools and school districts with the new curricula and set standards for achievement by grade level. The disequilibrium lay in the preparation and training involved for busy teachers and school leaders. The testing was very unpopular among teachers, as it represented additional work for teachers and at a critical learning time for children. The junior and primary team leaders, along with the vice-principal, coordinated the endeavor, were centrally trained, and then returned to train the teachers involved. Intermediate teachers gave their time to help supervise students.

The testing process was relatively successful, and it was encouraging to see how all the teachers pulled together to accomplish the task. When the school received the results of the provincial tests conducted the previous spring, the results revealed a major issue: the mathematics scores for Grade

3 French Immersion (FI) students were significantly lower than the norm for such students. Disequilibrium: The primary FI students were having difficulty understanding the math concepts taught in French.

The principal and vice-principal met with all the primary and junior-level teachers (English and French) to review how people were teaching math. The primary FI teachers indicated that their math-teaching methods were consistent with those of other division groups, but math was not a strong academic area for many of the primary teachers. The school was fortunate to have on-staff a former district math consultant who was also a co-chair of the math curriculum committee and one of the junior-level FI teachers.

Several collective decisions were made to attempt to rectify the situation. The consultant teacher was asked to further review the new math curriculum and design a series of workshops for all teachers to ensure consistency and understanding across the whole school. He received appropriate release time and thankful recognition from his colleagues for his efforts and abilities. In addition, with his permission, the timetable was altered so that he could directly teach math in French to the Grade 3 FI students every day.

This problem was approached by the teachers in all three divisions and for two languages. The final plan was a group solution, and from a Systems Thinking perspective, challenges are met through the strength of our connections with others. In the following years, planning for the testing was led by cross-division teams. The teachers better understood how to prepare themselves and their classes and how to assist identified students.

After the school's significant changes regarding math instruction, the next year's Grade 3 FI results increased to a significantly higher level, indicating that the strategies had been successful! In addition, all primary and junior division math results were significantly higher. When the results were announced, the school had great cause to celebrate. The school had changed the academic course of school progress in just two years! This celebration marked a distinct positive shift in the overall school attitude, climate, and energy.

The school now had developed well-established procedures and shared leadership opportunities for each of the two divisions. The preparation time for the teachers had been cut significantly, and the level of teacher, student, and parent anxiety also dissipated. Some parents and teachers commented that it appeared to run itself. Such a *Whole System Coherence* (WSC) is achieved when subsystems interact, interrelate, and collaborate to create a unified approach, and everybody working as one is essential for creating sustainable schools (Mann, 2023).

THE FINAL STEPS TO CREATING A NEW CULTURE, DISEQUILIBRIUM: TWO SCHOOLS, ONE BUILDING

Many schools in the district were troubled by a similar problem. Having a dual-track school with French Immersion from kindergarten through eighth grade and a parallel track for English programming caused a divisive problem for the school: *two schools in one*. There had always been pressure from many parents whose backgrounds were English or French to have their children learn French.

Often, the rigors of the FI curriculum caused less able FI students or students with learning disabilities to be discouraged from taking the FI pathway, and they would eventually drop out of the program after a year or two. There were no academic resources available to help FI students. This caused not only an issue about inclusivity but also created an "English academic ghetto" in Grades 7 and 8, with many students being identified as being "hard to teach."

The leadership team shared their ideas informally with other schools and the division leaders. There were district guidelines indicating the number of minutes that FI students had to be taught in French. After consulting formally with the faculty and school council concerning the school belief statement, all parties agreed to blend the two language groups for more of their classes. The changes went smoothly, and the school operated sustainably as a united system for another eight years after this decision.

When networks are recognized as a basic pattern of living in an organization, everything and everyone is connected in an interdependent web of interactions. Staying focused on the purpose of the network for sustainable learning keeps everyone moving in the right direction as leaders promote bonds with others (Scanga & Sedlack, 2023).

Everyday Disequilibrium

There are many successful daily examples of systems thinking applied to events or issues that occur in most schools in which observed disequilibrium motivates change. It is a matter of how one perceives an organization: as a system or a series of isolated events. The following are examples of "everyday issues" which can be viewed through a systems lens:

1. Fundraising events often are seen as stand-alone events, but they demonstrate how energetic teachers mobilize and motivate whole school communities for a cause;

2. Musicals, choirs, theatre productions, and concerts that occur regularly in most schools are viewed as summative arts demonstrations but are essential building blocks for the whole school community;
3. Parent-Teacher Interview Decisions are the type of school decision that could cause some disequilibrium. Often teachers suggest alternate approaches to reporting. For example, when several leaders, after training, support *Portfolio-based, Student-Led Parent-Teacher Interviews*, these conferences can be quite successful. Positive results can motivate other teachers to adopt different methods in the future.
4. Developing Social Help Programs, such as a *Peer Mediators Program* with the help of a local Police Liaison Officer, can reduce violence. The school can witness a significant improvement in school climate and a recorded reduction in playground violence. As a result, many students can become positive role models.
5. Every rewards assembly and every staff party should be considered a system celebration. Recognition given to students, teachers, and teams for their contributions promotes the value of every other group member. Most importantly, the collective recognizes the contributions of each member. "In a winning culture you understand and accept that other people are depending on you, and you behave accordingly" (Messier, 2021: p. 163). This is an opportunity for schools and teams to reach this recognizable level of *esprit de corps*.

YEAR FOUR: A CURRICULUM CASE STUDY REVIEW: ESPRIT DE CORPS AND CULTURE REALIZED

The school's test results in the previous three years showed consistent success from the programs and changes put in place to accommodate apparent disequilibrium. Purposive action can promote shared beliefs, attitudes, values, and behaviors that support sustainable learning that is ongoing (Acker-Hocevar, 2023).

Curriculum Review (Creating Disequilibrium)

With the accumulated successes buoying up organizational confidence, the next building step was proposed to the staff and school council. Rather than using the school's earlier curriculum process for implementation of the Language Arts (LA) curriculum, it was proposed that the school could honor the pathways taken by the teachers and review the school's progress over three years with the LA curriculum. The principal suggested a *Case Study Review*, which could be accomplished in a more focused but less-time-consuming approach over one month in the spring. After outlining the pros and cons, the school decided to use the case study method.

The case study was organized into three parts for data collection: 1) Focus Groups, 2) a Questionnaire, and 3) Provincial Test Results assessing students, teachers, and parents. The study would be led by an Internal Reviewer (a teacher from within the school) and an External Reviewer (a teacher selected from outside the school). The principal would serve as a guide for the process. Other teachers from each division volunteered to join the review team.

Focus groups represented each of the divisions for students, teachers, and parents and represented each grade level of FI and English instruction. The focus group questions referenced the language curriculum and were developed by the review committee. At each division level, group questions were very similar in intent and sequence. The questionnaires were developed from the results of the focus group responses and served to gather data and confirm the findings from and across those groups. Questionnaires were distributed randomly among parents, teachers, and students at each of the division levels and assessed by the reviewers.

Over three years, the Provincial Test Results for Language Arts were assessed for each division by the team responsible for the school's testing organization and compared with findings from other data collection teams. All data and findings were evaluated and synthesized by the reviewer team, and results were established for a report submitted to the staff, school council, and the superintendent in May of that year.

The results and report were pertinent to the school at the time and created some disequilibrium in each division. These findings were intended to be used the following year as a guide to review and plan the direction for the L.A. program, but colleagues working together became the binding strength of the exercise. The review evolved into an energy-producing, fact-finding inquiry that ultimately created information from which to move forward.

A CALL TO ACTION

As a leader in a school that builds energy systems, one must promote and embrace disequilibrium, build new alliances and networks to address emerging disruption, and encourage and enable novelty to engender and develop complex support systems. By building *systems thinking* into a school's growth process, energy emerges from within to promote momentum for responding to the changing context of work.

The stories of FB School have not been told sequentially but rather according to decisions that continuously changed the school culture and the people in it a little at a time through earned trust, foresight, collaboration, and team building. These could be the stories of decisions made in any suburban school in North America.

Schools are often faced with extraordinary decisions about life and death, mandated curriculum tasks, or personal tragedy. These are important issues that address how decisions are made and build school culture. The bottom line is that all decisions are important, and when made through a consistent and collaborative systems approach, they generate team trust, natural positive energy, and an exciting "esprit de corps" that shows a creative and caring school culture.

When the principal moved to the district office as superintendent, he began to operate with groups of principals as he had at the school level with *systems thinking* in mind. He presented disequilibrium to these groups involving curricular issues that were upcoming and had these leader groups organize and familiarize themselves with these issues and to plan an approach. The principal groups appreciated the autonomy of the collaborative work and grew more engaged and committed to the work and each other over the year.

This is the real work of a district superintendent team: seeing what disequilibrium lies ahead for the whole system and acting through principal work groups to prepare the district's schools for a consistent approach to issues at hand. The clear value added to using this networking strategy is that it brings principals together to purposefully work together and build support and collaboration among that leadership group. As well, as the process models practice for all school workers.

Principals and superintendents who want to build a successful, positive, and ethical school and district dynamic are highly encouraged to adopt a *Systems Thinking* approach to their organization. Schools must become encouraging and caring environments that respond naturally to the disequilibrium and solutions of everyday life to best prepare students for success.

REFERENCES

Acker-Hocevar, M. (2023). A quantum worldview of responsive power for sustainable learning. In K. J. Snyder & K. M. Snyder (Eds.), *Systems thinking for sustainable schooling: A mindshift for educators to lead and achieve quality in schools.* Lanham, MD: Rowman and Littlefield Publishers.

Acker-Hocevar, M., Cruz-Jansen, M. I., & Wilson, C. L. (2012). *Leadership from the ground up: Sustainable school improvement in traditionally low-performing schools.* Charlotte, NC: Information Age Publishers.

Fitzgerald, J. H., & Sullivan, E. C. (2023). Toward the school as a sustainable global learning center system. In K. J. Snyder & K. M. Snyder (Eds.), *Systems thinking for sustainable schooling: A mindshift for educators to lead and achieve quality in schools.* Lanham, Md: Rowman and Littlefield Publishers.

Hasenstab, J. (1989). *Project T.E.A.C.H.* Cadiz, KY: Performance Learning Systems Inc.

Mann, J. (2023). Appreciative school systems: A path to school success. In K. J. Snyder & K. M. Snyder (Eds.), *Systems thinking for sustainable schooling: A mindshift for educators to lead and achieve quality in schools.* Lanham, MD: Rowman and Littlefield Publishers.

Martensson, A., & Snyder, K. M. (2023). Approaching systems thinking in schools by linking quality and sustainability: Moving from Theory to Practice. In K. J. Snyder & K. M. Snyder (Eds.), *Systems thinking for sustainable schooling: A mindshift for educators to lead and achieve quality in schools.* Lanham, MD: Rowman and Littlefield Publishers

Messier, M., & Roberts, J. (2021) *No one wins alone: A Memoir.* Toronto: Simon and Schuster.

Scanga, D., & Sedlack, R. (2023). Networking for principal sustainability. In K. J. Snyder & K. M. Snyder (Eds.), *Systems thinking for sustainable schooling: A mindshift for educators to lead and achieve quality in schools.* Lanham, MD: Rowman and Littlefield Publishers

Snyder, K. J., (2023). Systems thinking and sustainable schooling: Foundations in physics, In K. J. Snyder & K. M. Snyder (Eds.), *Systems thinking for sustainable schooling: A mindshift for educators to lead and achieve quality in schools.* Lanham, MD: Rowman and Littlefield Publishers.

Snyder, K. J., Hocevar, M., & Snyder, K. M. (2008). *Living on the edge of Chaos: Leading schools into the global age.* Milwaukee, WI: ASQ Quality Press.

Snyder K. J., & R. Anderson. (1986). *Managing productive schools: Toward an ecology.* Orlando, FL: Academic Press.

Sullivan, E. C. (2023). The Quantum School Leader as a Strategic Systems Thinker. In K. J. Snyder & K. M. Snyder (Eds.), *Systems thinking for sustainable schooling: A mindshift for educators to lead and achieve quality in schools.* Lanham, MD: Rowman and Littlefield Publishers.

Chapter 7

(Re)imagined Teacher Learning and Improvement with Systems Thinking

Corbett Prep and Its "Culture of Fit"

Helen M. Hazi

Corbett Preparatory is a unique school where teachers learn and continuously improve without the teacher evaluation system that is typically used to determine teacher quality. Yet, everyone knows who the effective teachers are and whether they "fit." This chapter describes the "culture of fit," one of many that support continuous improvement for teachers as well as students. Educators may be interested in Corbett Prep, because US schools struggle to find ways to involve and support teachers in their learning and improvement, a difficult-to-accomplish goal.

This chapter is based on an on-campus visit and interviews of teachers and administrators at Corbett Prep during the period 2021–2022, information found on its website, and writings from those who have studied this independent day school. When teachers and administrators reviewed this chapter, they added a few details but otherwise thought it captured teaching and learning at Corbett Prep. One said, "Thanks for articulating 'fit' so well." Another said, "The chapter is wonderful! It beautifully captures our culture and the 'fit factor' of our faculty."

The author draws from systems thinking in physics and total quality management, and selected theory from teacher learning, improvement, and professional development. Concepts from each will be used to explain teachers and their culture of fit at Corbett. The chapter includes sections on the school's philosophy, professional development, teaming, how teachers determine "fit," that is, belonging at Corbett, and how administrators think about teaming and evaluation. The chapter ends with challenges and possibilities, with an eye on what educators can learn from these teachers.

THE SCHOOL'S PHILOSOPHY

Systems thinking is the interrelationship and interdependence of everything around a common purpose (Snyder, 2023). *In schools, learning is its mission, embodied in the actions of those working together for its common purpose* (Mårtensson & Snyder, 2023). Corbett Prep was founded in 1968 as a nonprofit, independent[1] day school by two teachers, supported with tuition and funding from special donors and the community. Its philosophy of learning and teaching has been largely influenced by Dr. Joyce Swarzman, an inner-city teacher and teacher educator[2] who was its headmaster for over 25 years.

Corbett's philosophy is:

> that a happy child . . . one who is . . . allowed to fulfil his/her needs to play, investigate and be him/herself . . . is more open to learning than a child who is unhappy, tense and fearful. We consider it our responsibility to foster each child's capacity for learning . . . individualizing each child's school experience. . . . [S]chool should be interesting and even exciting; that each child's work and behavior should be evaluated in terms of his/her inherent capacity, rather than through comparison with others; and that cooperation is more valuable than the competition. (Corbett Prep, 2022, "Philosophy")

It is a place where school is exciting, where students are capable of doing many things, and where mistakes are opportunities to improve (Cohen, 2003). To accomplish this, Corbett Prep, which evolved into a pre-K through 8th-grade school, has "one of the best, most highly trained faculties in the world" (Cohen, 2003, p. 5). Teachers are there because of their love for children, love of learning, and going the extra mile so that children can learn. Administrators are there to help teachers make their jobs easier.

Their philosophy for best practices is known as Multiple Options for Results in Education (M.O.R.E.).[3] According to Joyce, these "initiatives" became a way for administrators to first establish school routines, and then to control future initiatives. One or more teachers volunteer to investigate, train, and lead the initiative and then adapt, integrate, evaluate, and sustain it.

Teachers interviewed came to the school for a variety of reasons. One staff member who had worked in the office wanted to be part of the family and so became a teaching assistant while working toward her master's degree. One had moved to the area when a husband had relocated to a new job, while another moved there to take care of an elderly mother-in-law. Still another, encouraged by a trusted advisor, applied because she wanted to teach at an international school. When touring the campus, one applicant was impressed when she saw a teacher picking up trash and moving things around; she said, "She really cares about this school!"

Once these teachers joined Corbett, they experienced happy people, a sense of family, and individual fulfillment. One teacher said, "If you go to a place where people stay for a while, you tend to find happy people, who want to be there." "We don't have family nearby, but we have a family of learners, and for kids to grow up with the same groups of kids, and educators here," said another. Yet another reported, "I taught in isolation, and did lesson plans, emails, and everything by myself. I was an island. I became part of this community in not just kindergarten, but in every sense. Could not imagine leaving and teaching on an island."

Teachers stayed at the school for a number of reasons. One teacher wanted her children to be raised in an environment where they are "taught by multiple teachers and they experience cooperative learning and team teaching." Another said there was constant learning: "We are constantly changing, constantly growing. We are being made the life-long learners like we want our students to be." This theme of life-long learning is supported by Corbett's philosophy of professional development.

Professional Development

In systems thinking, the organization invests in developing and transforming its people in traditional (i.e., curriculum and instruction), *organizational* (to solve everyday problems such as scheduling and parent communication) *and transformative skills* (new curriculum and best practices) that allow the organization to respond to disruptions, then grow and innovate (Lilja et al., 2022). Professional development is a priority for teachers and takes multiple forms.

New teachers receive five days of training prior to the start of school, and their induction continues throughout the year in the team they join. In fact, team members participate in their interviews. All teachers have a daily planning period of 60 minutes; two hours for training and meetings every Tuesday; one half day monthly for in-service; and professional conferences throughout the school year. Training is guided by research-based learning strategies, programs recognized by national educational associations, and "best practices" (Cohen, 2003). It also invites educators worldwide to visit campus for professional development.

M.O.R.E. is "how we do things here," and reflects their philosophy of teaching and professional development. They "create a brain-friendly environment to accelerate the learning process." In fact, two of the teachers interviewed were on a committee revisiting M.O.R.E. because it was "dense," and "new teachers would be overwhelmed."

Teaming

In systems thinking, teaming[4] is "a way of working that brings people together to generate new ideas, find answers, and solve problems" (Edmondson, 2012, p. 24). Corbett has various levels of teams that combine and recombine within and across grade levels, within and across subjects and divisions, and within and outside of the school. Corbett Prep teams have developed relationships with teachers in other countries, and the administrators attribute the school's innovation, many achievements, and awards to teaming (Anderson, 2023).

Robert Anderson introduced team teaching to Corbett Prep over 25 years ago under the leadership of Joyce Swarzman. Team teaching had been promoted along with non-gradedness at Harvard University's School of Education in the 1950s and 1960s to promote professional flexibility and resources for teaching in the learning environment. It became an alternative to the age-graded grouping of students, who were expected to function academically within the same grade level, and where teachers taught standardized curriculum in self-contained classrooms, independent of their colleagues (Anderson, 2023).

According to Anderson (2023), teams of four to six elementary and middle school teachers share responsibilities for teaching multi-age groups of children. Teaming provided professional company, professional development, and induction for those newly hired teachers. While it became popular in places such as Corbett, teachers elsewhere were resistant because they lost their privacy and independence and could not ignore the difficult student or difficult-to-teach curriculum. With teaming, teachers could flexibly teach individuals and small groups to best meet student needs and to teach to their strengths while observing other teachers do the same.

Those interviewed said teaching in a team was "almost like one brain. We finish each other's sentences. . . . It's like a dance" and "Love having a partner to work with. I spend more time with her than with my own husband and children. We fight like we're a married couple." Another said, "We complement each other. No one is the leader. Everyone takes leadership on different parts based on what they do best. I'm not as good alone, as the three of us together." Still, another said, "It's like a think tank where everyone actively shares. Everyone has respect for each other. Everyone has everyone else's back. We help each other."

At one point during the interview, one teacher shared the name of a teacher who was returning to Corbett to be part of her team. Two of them who knew the teacher smiled, excited about who would rejoin them in the fall. This illustrates that teacher-teacher relationships are important at Corbett.

It also appears as if the teachers who were interviewed view teaming and evaluation as linked: "We had our teammates keeping us in check. Very different. Better than that [annual evaluation] because it's continuous."

EVALUATION BY "FIT"

In systems thinking, organizations are learning cultures in which their employees are given feedback for continuous improvement, one of the cornerstones of Quality Management, *so that they can grow* (Mårtensson & Snyder, 2023). A most interesting aspect of this study was that administrators, teachers, and even a board member were adamant that teachers were not evaluated, even though such a policy was required for accreditation (FCIS, 2021)!

While the school reported for accreditation purposes that teacher evaluation was self-assessment and a conference with the principal, Joyce chose not to meet with teachers. Instead, teachers decided on their own if they "fit" at Corbett and would leave of their own volition, according to Joyce. And in the early years, when some did not want to use Tuesdays to sharpen their skills, they did (Cohen, 2003). These were teachers who worked in silos or moved away. A few, who left for the public schools, returned when they realized that at Corbett, they were free from surveillance and regulation.

While those interviewed never used the word "evaluate," teachers eventually came to talk about evaluation as "fit." Teachers interviewed used phrases such as "teachers keep us in check," "we are coached," "Joyce micro-analyzed everything," and "it wasn't 'criticism' but a matter of perspective." Teachers also said that when Joyce came into the room, they thought "O.K. We're going to be coached again and we're to say 'Thank you for the coaching,' smile, then implement what she told you."

One teacher reported: "If you took it personally or got upset because someone was telling you what to do, and you already know everything. People would get very upset and end up just quitting. They called it 'getting criticized.' It's two words: you're either being coached or criticized. It's a mindset. People would quit because they got frustrated with Joyce and their teammates who would tell them what to do. It was meant to be for growth. . . . Some people have a lock on their brain. I never felt like I was a master teacher. I'm learning every day."

Another teacher reported that it might take time for teachers new to a team to figure out if they fit, especially if they assume they know what is going on with the children or a lesson: "It was interesting when people realized this was not the place for them. Some people realized it quickly, sometimes they didn't. I've had a couple hired as assistants and they had trouble. [They think] 'I really know how to do this, and do that.' [But] they haven't understood this growth idea. You actually don't know what's going on in this place. It's surprising to them."

In reflection after the interview, one teacher defined "fit" in the form of questions: "Does this person fit . . . or will they change to fit? . . . It is never about liking someone. . . . Does this particular position suit the person and are they carrying their weight and committed to the team's success?" To be successful at Corbett, the teacher added, "A person who grows and adapts will succeed and improve."

Some also saw the team's evaluation as evolving, where in the beginning, "it could be hostile, but it takes time like a marriage to fall into that rhythmic dance . . . it was much more [like] a superior evalua[ting]." Another teacher reported that "it took us about six years to where we are right now" to function as a team. Yet another offered: "Teaming is evaluating all day long, every day, in real-time, and on the spot."

In a later conversation, Joyce said she used "Plus-Delta," a formative evaluation that provides feedback on an experience or event and collects ideas for future improvements. It is framed in 'improvement' language rather than language that might be experienced negatively. The plus identified what went well. The delta identifies what might be changed to improve a process or activity ("What is plus delta evaluation," 2022, para. 1).

Closely allied with the culture of "fit" is the culture of "mistake." Joyce tells the story that when a child with a test in hand approached as she walked on campus, she asked "What do you have there?" The boy looked up and said shyly, "My test. I didn't do so good!" Then Joyce replied, "That's a mistake. And how do we fix that?" When the boy gave the correct answer, she praised him. Teachers said that Joyce wanted them to use positive phrasing for all communication and to make it another opportunity to learn. "That's the way it works with us. You're always improving," said one teacher.

Its Administrators

The "culture of fit" would be incomplete without the administrators' point of view. Corbett administrators support teaming when they hire and place teachers, allot time in the schedule for their meetings, and help the weaker links. These practices are found in the research that has rediscovered the value of teaming (Johnson, 2021).

Teaming has become a central component of school-wide improvement. Administrators recognize that teaming is important to the school's continued growth and sustainability. The headmaster has an administrative team and an expanded leadership team, including heads of teams and divisions.

Recognizing he "can't do it all," the headmaster knows his strengths and "distributes" the leadership (Spillane et al., 2003) among those with the will and skill to identify needs and new initiatives.

Principals rigorously screen candidates and look "for a growth mindset and a readiness to collaborate" (Johnson et al., 2016, p. 28). Hiring starts in January with individual teacher meetings to determine what they'd like to do next year. Teachers identify conferences and meetings to attend for projects they lead. The headmaster works on the teams in February, and annual contract talks are in March and April. Since many teachers are long-established and skilled, the headmaster likes to keep them where they are for consistency of the curriculum and to induct those new to the school so they are successful. He also knows when the school needs to grow.

Three stories illustrate the headmaster's strategy for team sustainability (Snyder & Snyder, 2021). The current headmaster told the story of one academically strong team's need for someone to clean up, decorate, and help with the bathroom. "I wouldn't admit students," he said, "unless I had the best team to support them." In the first days of school, he found that aid, then admitted the students. Another team needed someone with a strong academic background for learning centers and could adjust on-the-fly. The headmaster also wanted someone "warm and fuzzy" to connect with both students and their parents. He found that teacher, too!

He told another story about a twenty-plus-year teacher with a school history and content knowledge but who went through five partners in seven years. This year, she is a division leader, coordinating and redirecting her energy to help teachers grow. He also gave teachers special assignments in curriculum and well-being and added a Student Success Team, knowing that accreditation was near and that the pandemic had left some children weak in certain skills.

Principals protect team time, attend their meetings, and use their work to support teachers across the school (Johnson et al., 2016). Meetings are essential for teaming to work at Corbett. The headmaster thought the many configurations of teams were so important that he appointed one teacher to schedule school-wide events, individual planning periods, monthly school-wide meetings, meetings with divisions, and vertical (subject) and horizontal (grade) teams. Their time ranges from 45 to 90 minutes. Before events are finalized, teams will review, confirm or change the year-at-a-glance with different colored sticky notes spanning four walls.

Administrators add value to the "culture of fit." While they want teachers to contribute to the team and have a growth mindset, they also look at personality and their connection to students outside the classroom. When questioned, the headmaster said that personality does matter "when you have to take complaints from 'the high flyers' who have to support 'the weaker link.'" The headmaster knows whom each are, citing a number from last year and this year. He reported that he first looks to move the weak link to another team or role that builds on strength, or provide support before encouraging anyone to leave the school.

Principals frequently observe, provide written feedback, and support the weaker link so a team "did not bear full responsibility for individual teachers' improvement" (Johnson et al., 2016, p. 28). The headmaster believes it's important to be "out there and in classrooms most of the day, but my job in [the office] starts at 4:30." He leaves a positive on a sticky note after he observes, wants more eyes in the classroom for those "coachable moments," and wants teachers to share a "wow moment" with the whole faculty.

One principal likes to co-teach and use the Plus-Delta. Once teams gel in the middle school, she wants teams to observe other teachers, have conferences, and set goals for more mastery learning and individualized inquiry-based instruction.

As Corbett Prep prepares for accreditation, administrators are contemplating what to do with evaluation. It's hard these days *not* to be influenced by 72 item observation rubrics from internationally recognized educators. Some may feel it gives them credibility with teachers. However, at its core, the "culture of fit" works at Corbett Prep for both teachers and administrators. Administrators may just need to believe that they *can* "dance to a different beat," yet help those "weaker links" leave—the ones who start their day at 7:30 and leave at 3:30.

OPPORTUNITIES AND CHALLENGES

As educators face school shootings and cultural tensions in communities, morale is at an all-time low as teachers leave and create shortages (e.g., Will, 2022). At the same time, some are rediscovering that teaming results in more student and teacher satisfaction, improved lesson quality, and increased collaboration and flexibility in staffing (Chen & Banchero, 2022). "Teaming elevates the level of being a teacher," said one teacher. Indeed, Corbett Prep must be doing a few things right, if the majority of the teaching staff has been at the school for more than five years, and in many more cases, more than 10 to 15 years (Mårtensson & Snyder, 2023).

According to Rouse (2021), employee retention is an understudied topic due to the focus on high turnover rates. "Employees are likely to stay with an organization when they are engaged, have job satisfaction and have additional tools of access to training and development" (Rouse, 2021, p. 5). Teachers at Corbett have time during the day, week, and month for professional development and have opportunities to travel nationally and internationally with initiatives they lead.⁵

In most US public schools, the teacher evaluation instrument is the common language for evaluators and teachers to discuss teaching and instructional feedback (Kraft & Gilmour, 2016). Not so at Corbett Prep—it's M.O.R.E. Horn and Kane (2019, p. 121) believe teachers need "consistent and precise terminology for referring to the core participants, activities, and materials of teaching and learning." In turn, "teachers' workplace conversations support their professional learning" (p. 121). Lefstein et al. (2020) call this *pedagogically productive talk* that shapes the way teachers think about and see their teaching.

M.O.R.E. beliefs and pedagogical practices are first learned when teachers new to the school are inducted, reinforced in in-service professional development, and then used daily by teachers in teams and administrators when coaching. Furthermore, they are used to communicate with parents. Over time M.O.R.E became normalized, tacit, and embedded in the school culture. Lefstein et al. (2020, p. 361) assert that "work-based discussions are likely to be more influential" in shaping teachers' expectations and practice. This, in part, may help explain why teachers view the team as consequential to determining "fit."

Learning and teaching are its core systems. The philosophy that guides students and their learning is the same that guides teachers and their learning. Teachers work together to achieve the desired goals in a culture necessary to sustain quality (Mårtensson & Snyder, 2023). Joyce Swarzman seems to have treated Corbett Prep as a professional practice school where she could induct new teachers into the profession, build and sustain the best educational practices, and "provide for continuing development and professional growth of experienced in-service teachers" (Lieberman & Miller, 1990, p.105).

Borko (2004, p. 3) reveals that "the professional development currently available to teachers is woefully inadequate," costs billions of dollars that is "fragmented, intellectually superficial, and do[es] not take into account what we know about how teachers learn." Yet professional development at Corbett is a regular routine—daily, weekly, and monthly.

"Teacher evaluation" by this name does *not* exist at Corbett Prep, yet teachers and administrators experience it as whether they "fit." In what I call the "culture of fit," teachers are "kept in-check," "coached," and "micro-analyzed" by other teachers, who describe it as a "mindset" or "perspective" and the "Olympic Mentality." "Joyce would say it's the best getting better," said one teacher, "standing on the shoulders of those who've come before us." Most importantly, teachers come to understand whether or not they belong at this school.

While teams evaluate whether teachers belong, so do teachers, though not much was mentioned about self-evaluation, which has "historically ... been of little value. Most dismiss it as a strategy of self-improvement that is fraught with problems" (Barber, 1991, p. 216).[6] Teachers at Corbett Prep have *peer-assisted self-evaluation* in which team members provide continuous—even daily—feedback where "a teacher must first admit that he or she is doing something less than perfectly and that the teacher's behavior can be improved" (p. 216).

Teachers also learn from students' reactions to their instruction and their mistakes, making "in the moment decisions" (Schelling & Rubenstein, 2021). One teacher shared, "Our lessons have benchmarks and are successful when we meet or exceed them with as many students as possible. . . . We observe the lesson in progress and make mid-course corrections to reflect the situation of the students we have, rather than the situation we expected."

Another added, "Each lesson is differentiated, and students work toward mastery. Lessons are not tweaked at the end. They are tweaked along the way so that every student has the chance to be successful and achieve mastery. This constant revision helps the students be successful and show mastery when the final assessment is given."

Warner (2021) believes that learning from mistakes is essential to becoming a better teacher. By framing an action or result as a mistake, the teacher can lean into the discomfort of deeply examining, understanding, and then embracing it. It is quite different from striving to be the perfect teacher, where one shallowly reflects and then hides failure from others. Teaming makes this impossible, yet it also helps them correct and learn from mistakes.

A CALL TO ACTION

After two decades of state activity and billions of dollars invested in complex and rigorous evaluation systems in the United States, a recent study showed that teacher evaluation had no discernible effect on student achievement in the states (Bleiberg et al., 2021). Still, advocates for teacher quality remain hopeful that "teacher evaluation [reform], when well-implemented . . . is . . . possible" (Will, 2021, para. 30) with more buy-in and time to address challenges of implementation.

Can I imagine a future where there are no teacher evaluations? Yes, but not everywhere. Further study of Corbett Prep may reveal why teams and the culture of "fit" work. This inquiry hints at long-established cultures of learning, mistakes, continuous improvement, teaming, and professional development that are all support systems that sustain quality teachers. Teachers, students, and administrators are all interconnected around a common purpose—facilitating each other's learning and growth (Snyder & Snyder, 2021).

But like the underwhelming results of studying effective schools, learning what makes a school effective does not guarantee that ineffective schools can become effective by adopting those same qualities. There can be different types of teacher and administrator teams, undertaking different types of work, under administrators with different styles, but all must have similar values and work in harmony as one, united in purpose.

Instead, we can learn that those quality teachers who do "fit" seem to thrive. Two teachers say what they get from Corbett: "I need to be supported by my colleagues and management and be allowed to support them, listened to, invited to give my opinions, given the authority to do things and then allowed to do them. Give and receive constructive advice, be mentored, and trusted to mentor."

Another teacher said, "Trust is felt everywhere at Corbett. I have autonomy over my classroom, am able to lead events, and my opinions are listened to and valued. I am greeted with a smile. My principal has an open-door policy—she will make time to meet with me at a moment's notice, and if not then, she will schedule a time that is usually the same day."

Ford et al. (2018, p. 6), who have studied and are skeptical of teacher evaluation systems, believe that "for teachers, having autonomy, meaningful relationships with colleagues and students, and seeing their hard work pay off in student success are all key psychic rewards." Every learner should have the freedom to experiment, bounce ideas off of colleagues, and be supported by those who want them to be successful. So should every teacher.

NOTES

This chapter is dedicated to the teachers who met with me and responded to a draft of this chapter. Ashley, Cynthia, Kathryn, John, Jen, Lauren, Linda, and Michael are dedicated to their students and make Corbett Prep the successful and magical place that it is! Thanks, too, to Nick, Jenn, and Mike, who make it all possible.

1. Independent or private schools "are independent in philosophy driven by a unique mission, an independent board of trustees, and primarily supported through tuition payments and charitable contributions. They are accountable to their communities and accrediting bodies" (Johnson, 2021, p. 4). There are 34,576 (10%) private schools in the United States serving 5.7 million (25%) pre–12 students.

2. Swarzman trained over 10,000 educators in the Suncoast Area Teacher Training Program at the University of South Florida, one of the most innovative and research-based teacher training programs in the country, where its graduates were known for being highly skilled and innovative. While at Corbett, she trained another 10,000 teachers locally and internationally. She has received numerous awards,

including the prestigious 2021 Edgar McCleary Service Award, from the Florida Council of Independent Schools.

3. Some are dispositions (e.g., the Olympic Mindset, Yale's RULER program, The Contentment Foundation's Wellbeing Program, positive communications, social emotional learning), curriculum (e.g., International Baccalaureate, STEAM), teaching methods (e.g., Kagan's cooperative learning, learning styles, and multiple intelligences), and those that are a combination (e.g., emotional intelligence, brain-based learning). Some initiatives are typical of schools (e.g., field trips, community service), but others are innovative (e.g., international exchange of students and teachers) (M.O.R.E, 2022; Snyder, 2007).

4. While "teaming" is a concept that has emerged within educational systems, it connects to the system's concepts of interconnectivity and networking (Snyder, 2023).

5. An endowment has been recently established to honor Dr. Swarzman, who calls herself "a workshop junkie," to continue to promote teacher professional development. In addition, three teachers and one administrator are pursuing doctoral study at Mid Sweden University directed by Dr. Kristen Snyder, with the mentorship of Dr. Karolyn Snyder, a board member. Dr. Swarzman views this doctoral program to be the crowning achievement of her efforts to professionalize teachers.

6. All four handbooks of teacher evaluation include a chapter on or refer to self-assessment or evaluation (Millman, 1981; Millman & Darling-Hammond, 1991; Kennedy, 2010; Stronge & Tucker, 2003).

REFERENCES

Anderson, R. (2023). The beginnings of collaboration schools: Team teaching and multi-age grouping. In K. J. Snyder & K. M. Snyder (Eds.), *Systems thinking for sustainable schooling: A mindshift for educators to lead and achieve quality in schools.* Lanham, MD: Rowman & Littlefield.

Barber, L. (1991). Self-assessment. In L. Darling-Hammond & J. Millman (Eds.), *Handbook of teacher evaluation* (pp. 216–228). Sage Publications.

Bleiberg, J., Brunner, E., Harbatkin, E., Kraft, M., & Springer, M. (2021, December). *The effect of teacher evaluation on achievement and attainment: Evidence from statewide reforms.* (EdWorkingPaper: 21–496) Annenberg Institute. https://www.edworkingpapers.com/ai21-496

Borko, H. (2004). Professional development and teacher learning: Mapping the terrain. *Educational Researcher*, 33(8), 3–15. https://doi.org/10.3102/0013189X033008003

Chen, I., & Banchero, S. (2022, July 20). It's time to rethink the 'one teacher, one classroom' model. *Education Week.* https://www.edweek.org/teaching-learning/opinion-its-time-to-rethink-one-teacher-one-classroom-model

Cohen, D. (2003). *It's all about kids: Every child deserves a 'teacher of the year.'* Be Happy Publishing.

Corbett Prep. (2022, July 21). Philosophy and mission. https://www.corbettprep.com/about/philosophy-and-mission

Edmondson, A. C. (2012). *Teaming: How organizations learn, innovate, and compete in the knowledge economy*. HB Printing.

Florida Council of Independent Schools. (2021, June). *FCIS Manual for evaluation and accreditation*. https://www.fcis.org/accreditation/resources-for-schools

Ford, T., Urick, A., & Wilson, A. (2018). Exploring the effect of supportive teacher evaluation experiences on U.S. teachers' job satisfaction. *Education Policy Analysis Archives*, 26(59), 1–36. http://dx.doi.org/10.14507/epaa.26.3559

Horn, I. S., & Kane, B. D. (2019). What we mean when we talk about teaching: The limits of professional language and possibilities for professionalizing discourse in teachers' conversations. *Teachers College Record*, 121(6), 1–32. https://doi.org/10.1177/016146811912100604

Johnson, M. (2021, July 13–15). How can school leaders leverage perceived and attractive quality to increase customer value to ensure organizational ability? In C. Johansson and V. Mauerhofer (Eds.), *Proceedings of the 27th annual conference, International Sustainable Development Research Society: Accelerating the progress towards the 2030 SDGs in times of crisis* (pp. 2079–2105). Mid Sweden University. http://miun.diva-portal.org/smash/get/diva2:1608600/FULLTEXT01.pdf

Johnson, S. M. (2021). Why teacher teams are more critical than ever. *Educational Leadership*, 79(1), 59–63. https://www.ascd.org/el/articles/why-teacher-teams-are-more-critical-than-ever

Johnson, S. M., Reinhorn, S., & Simon, N. (2016). Team work: Time well spent. *Educational Leadership*, 73(8), 24–29. https://www.ascd.org/el/articles/team-work-time-well-spent

Kennedy, M. (2010). *Teacher assessment and the quest for teacher quality: A handbook*. Jossey-Bass.

Kraft, M., & Gilmour, A. (2016). Can principals promote teacher development as evaluators? A case study of principals' views and experiences. *Educational Administration Quarterly*, 52(5), 711–753. https://doi.org/10.1177/0013161X16653445

Lefstein, A., Vedder-Weiss, D., & Segal, A. (2020). Relocating research on teacher learning: Toward pedagogically productive talk. *Educational Researcher*, 49(5), 360–368. https://doi.org/10.3102/0013189X20922998

Lieberman, A., & Miller, L. (1990). Teacher development in professional practice schools. *Teachers College Record*, 92(1), 105–122. https://doi.org/10.1177/016146819009200106

Lilja, J., Snyder, K., & Sten, L-M. (2022, June 15–17). Teaming for quality in the VUCA landscape: Exploring key elements for a next progressive leap in team-based practices to drive quality, sustainability, and regeneration. A paper presented at the 28th International Sustainable Development Research Society Conference, Stockholm.

Mårtensson, A., & Snyder, K. (2023). Approaching system thinking in schools by linking quality and sustainability: Moving from theory to practice. In K. J. Snyder & K. M. Snyder (Eds.), *Systems thinking for sustainable schooling: A mindshift for educators to lead and achieve quality in schools*. Rowman & Littlefield.

Millman. J. (1981). *Handbook of teacher evaluation*. Sage Publications.

Millman, J., & Darling-Hammond, L. (1991). *The new handbook of teacher evaluation: Assessing elementary and secondary school teachers.* Corwin Press.

Multiple Options for Results in Education (M.O.R.E.). (2022, July 27). https://www.corbettprep.com/about/more-model

Rouse, K. S. (2021). 'Sticking power': Finding quality in organizational culture and employee wellbeing influencing an intention to stay. In J. F. Silva Gomes & S. A. Meguid (Eds.), Proceedings of the 9th International Conference on Mechanics and Materials in Design. https://paginas.fe.up.pt/~m2d/proceedings_m2d2022/data/papers/19123.pdf

Schelling, N., & Rubenstein, L. (2021). Elementary teachers' perceptions of data-driven decision making. *Educational Assessment, Evaluation and Accountability*, 33(2), 317–344. https://doi.org/10.1007/s11092-021-09356-w

Snyder, K. J. (2007). Why does IDS commit to M.O.R.E.? A two-page brochure. In Necessary conditions for student learning: An example for 20th century Learning.

Snyder, K. J. (2023). Systems thinking and sustainable schooling: Foundations in physics. In K. J. Snyder & K. M. Snyder (Eds.), *Systems thinking for sustainable schooling: A mindshift for educators to lead and achieve quality in schools.* Rowman & Littlefield.

Snyder, K. J., & Snyder, K. (2021, July 13–15). The human networked organization: Toward contemporary quality management and sustainability. A paper presented at the 27th International Sustainable Development Research Society Conference, Mid Sweden University. http://miun.diva-portal.org/smash/get/diva2:1608600/FULLTEXT01.pdf

Spillane, J., Diamond, J., & Loyiso, J. (2003). Leading instruction: The distribution of leadership for instruction. *Journal of Curriculum Studies*, 35(5), 533–543. https://doi.org/10.1080/0022027021000041972

Stronge, J., & Tucker, P. (2003). *Handbook on teacher evaluation: Assessing and improving performance.* Eye on Education.

Warner, J. (2021). *Failure before success: Teachers describe what they learned from mistakes.* Rowman & Littlefield.

What is delta-plus evaluation. (2022, July 27). *IGI global online dictionary.* https://www.igi-global.com/dictionary/plus-delta-evaluation/22865

Will, M. (2021, November). Efforts to toughen teacher evaluations show no positive impact on students. *Education Week.* https://www.edweek.org/teaching-learning/efforts-to-toughen-teacher-evaluations-show-no-positive-impact-on-students/2021/11

Will, M. (2022, April 15). "Disrespected" and "dissatisfied": 8 Takeaways from a new survey of teachers. *Education Week.* https://www.aft.org/press-release/under-siege-survey-teachers-finds-34-point-increase-job-dissatisfaction

Chapter 8

Complexity Thinking as a Way of Living to Develop Sustainable Schooling

Elaine C. Sullivan and John Fitzgerald

Schooling is becoming more complex, causing educators to grapple with how to prepare students for handling complex challenges that have developed with globalization. Among the skills needed are critical thinking, systems thinking, and strategic thinking (Redman & Wiek, 2021; Rieckmann, 2018). The challenge for educators is to link global learning to student activities. Complexity theorists suggest that complexity thinking skills can help educators address this challenge. Complexity thinking in education aims to understand complex systems and their capacity to show patterns, order, and structure in educational activities (Harmat & Herbert, 2020).

The International School Connection (ISC), a network of educators committed to developing schools as Global Learning Centers, advocates creating systems to integrate global issues in the teaching and learning of students and staff. Fitzgerald and Sullivan (2023) shared the ISC story of development over 25 years to help schools become global learning centers. The comprehensive model, called the ISC Global Learning Center Platform for Sustainable Schooling, integrates a school development approach using global learning benchmarks based on systems thinking and complexity.

In this chapter, the reader is guided deeper into the model by exploring an integration project of the ISC's Global Learning Benchmarks (GLBs) in the school curriculum and learning activities to illustrate how educators can redesign schools from a systems perspective to prepare youth as complexity thinkers. The Global Learning Platform integrates global knowledge into the learning environment instead of adding stand-alone programs. The systems approach is critical to sustaining education and is aligned with the UN Priority Action Area 2's research on change processes promoting an integration strategy of whole school change to transform schooling effectively (UNESCO, 2017; 2020).

The Global Learning Benchmark Integration Project, designed by the International School Connection, was initiated in a school in Tampa, Florida. The project reflects an evolution of the ISC's awareness of the need to help educators develop knowledge to think differently about learning in an age of globalization and complexity. Too many schools remain stuck in a silo-thinking mentality based on models from the industrial age. Systems thinking and complexity theory illustrate the importance of connecting the different functions within a school to create sustainable teaching and learning environments (Snyder et al., 2008).

This chapter is one about thinking. The concept of complexity thinking provides educators with an understanding of how to think differently for leading schools from a systems perspective. Readers will learn how to integrate global priorities into the daily fabric of the school through the Global Learning Platform that illustrates complexity thinking. These components are woven together in the final section to discuss developing sustainable schooling.

COMPLEXITY SHAPES A DIFFERENT MENTAL MODEL FOR FACILITATING CHANGE

Individuals must be change agents to create the world in which they wish to live and work. Complex thinking capabilities are among the key competencies for thriving today and contribute to resilience, adaptivity, and innovation (Brown, 2019). Acting as a complexity thinker allows one to analyze situations in which multiple systems interact. It can help us to live with the pervasive impacts of the growing complex challenges or opportunities affecting daily living.

A complex issue is a problem that does not have one right answer to fix it. Sometimes, there are too many factors, perhaps unknown, and they can change rapidly (Merali & Allen, 2011; Snowden, 2020). Complexity thinking (Harmat & Herbert, 2020) is a different mindset from those used to solve problems in the Industrial Age. Complexity thinking mirrors how living systems adapt to rapidly changing contexts (Teixeira de Melo, 2020). A globally oriented complexity-thinking perspective uses systems analysis to problem solve for adapting to complex issues for the well-being of the individual, the system, and society.

Complexity thinking is a concept derived from complexity theory and systems thinking (Capris & Luisi, 2014; Merali & Allen, 2011). It reflects a relational system of interactive parts that are non-linear. The interactions emerge through self-organization, cognition, co-evolution, and feedback to inform the dynamics of the thinking system. In organizational theory, this is used to re-imagine organizations as living systems. These interactions are relational and iterative, resulting in new information that disturbs the system, which causes different patterns to emerge, making complex thinking dynamic (Teixeira de Melo, 2020).

"Complexity Thinking as a Way of Living" is a daily mindset for holistic thinking to critically analyze systems for solving problems. A complexity mindset enables one to see the connectedness of a person's systems and helps to make sense of the interactions of their larger social systems (Snowden, 2020). The interactions of relationships highlight the entanglement of systems and people, and this entanglement requires individuals to use multiple perspectives in their thinking scheme to solve problems because diversity ensures access to the information and energy of the whole system (Wessels et al., 2022).

Complexity Thinking as a Way of Living can empower individuals to think critically about what possibilities might emerge to influence change for making a difference individually and collectively. The ISC links values, attitudes, and volition to develop complex thinking capabilities. Because the ISC stresses the relationships of people and context as part of how to think about systems, it helps a person interpret why unexpected and maybe unwanted conditions, such as globalization and technology, might impact their life.

Educators can use complexity thinking to create conditions to prepare students differently by thinking of a school as a living system, which aids in explaining the dynamics of social systems as complex adaptive systems that respond to change through their relationships and self-organization. A living system's relationship with its context offers other ways to think about managing and leading change processes (Capra & Luisi, 2014; Wheatley, 2017). This way of thinking can help educators align learning and teaching systems to become sustainable in an age of globalization.

UNESCO calls for a fundamental change in how to think about education's role in global development. According to UNESCO's general director, Irina Bokova (UN News: Global perspective human stories, 2014), education is a catalyst to impact the well-being of individuals and the future of our planet. Her comments suggest that education has a responsibility to align with global challenges and help youth develop the skills and values for leading a sustainable future. Viewing schools as a living system suggests that the internal systems of learning are dynamically related to external systems of the planet and society (Snyder et al., 2008).

The focus for globalizing the learning environment is to emphasize the interconnections and interdependencies of the system elements. The mutual connectedness and dependency of the parts create a perspective of understanding and thinking with a global worldview. The ISCs Strategic School Development approach uses complexity thinking and systems tools to create adaptive change aligned with the global imperative to transform education (Snyder et al., 2008; Sullivan, 2019).

THE ISC GLOBAL LEARNING PLATFORM CHARACTERIZES THE WORLD'S COMPLEX CONTEXT

The school's challenge is to link global learning into the fabric of school life every day! To support this need, the ISC created the Global Learning Platform (Snyder, 2019; Sullivan, 2019) to provide educators with the knowledge and examples for creating a global lens to frame their thinking about facilitating change in schools. The platform can help align the learning environment with the global context to build citizenship and competence for a sustainable future.

The Global Learning Platform integrates and operationalizes key concepts, indicators, and target goals from the various global frameworks. This integration provides a reference point for shaping the dimensions of student global competency and contributes to a student's knowledge of what it can look and feel like to be a capable global citizen. The elements of the platform are the Global Learning Benchmarks, the UN's Sustainable Development Goal (SDGs), the Program International Student Assessment (PISA) global competence domains, and UNESCO global citizenship standards.

UN Agenda 2030

The UN defines sustainability as the way of thinking about the future when pursuing development, such as economic growth, and improving situations in which environmental, economic, and social considerations are balanced (Brundtland, 1987). The UN 2030 Agenda identifies the 17 SDGs as the priority challenges to be addressed for transforming into a sustainable world (UNESCO, 2017). The 17 goals are grouped into priority areas and illustrated in Textbox 8.1. The SDGs targets and indicators provide information for acting and measuring progress toward reaching sustainability (UNESCO, 2020).

> **TEXTBOX 8.1. UN SUSTAINABLE DEVELOPMENT GOALS**
>
> 1. No Poverty, 2. Zero Hunger, 3. Good Health and Well-being, 4. Quality Education, 5. Gender Equity, 6. Clean Water and Sanitation, 7. Affordable, Clean Energy, 8. Decent Work & Economic Growth, 9. Industry, Innovation, & Infrastructure, 10. Reducing Inequality, 11. Sustainable Cities & Communities, 12. Responsible Consumption & Production, 13. Climate Action, 14. Life Below Water, 15. Life on Land, 16. Peace Justice & Strong Institution, and 17. Partnerships for the Goals
> (UN Department of Economic and Social Affairs, n.d.)

UNESCO Education Priority Action Areas

Global citizenship is UNESCO's umbrella term for individuals and communities as globally minded citizens who take action for environmental, political, and economic social equity and sustainability for all (UN Academic Impact, n.d.). The UN designates UNESCO (2017) to lead and assist educators in forming sustainable educational systems and programs to build global citizenship. A priority for education is to develop an individual's knowledge, skills, values, attitudes, and behaviors that allow them to assume active roles locally, nationally, and globally to shape a peaceful, just, and sustainable world (UN Academic Impact, n.d.).

UNESCO's educational council developed Priority Action Areas 2, 3, and 4 to increase education's role in preparing youth as change agents for building a sustainable and equitable world. Priority Action Area 2 is transforming the learning environments to prepare for global living. Priority Action Area 3 is building the capacities of educators to have a global mindset. Priority Action Area 4 identifies youth as the key actors in addressing future global challenges (UNESCO, 2020). The ISC uses a whole school change system, supported by Priority Action Area 2, to transform the learning environment to prepare students. Systems thinking tools facilitate the change process.

OECD/PISA Global Competence Domain

The Organization for Economic Co-operation and Development, through its findings of the Program for International Student Assessment (PISA), emphasizes that for individuals to thrive in our changing world, they must develop global competence for a 21st-century workforce (OECD, 2018). OECD/PISA points out that "globally competent individuals can examine local, global and intercultural issues, understand and appreciate different perspectives and world views, interact successfully and respectfully with others, and take responsible action toward sustainability and collective well-being" (Piacentini et al., 2017: p. 4).

PISA supports OECD's goal to produce an evolving competent workforce and global citizenship (OECD, 2018). The OECD emphasizes that the global connections within the world society are so prevalent, dense, complex, and quickly changing that being a globally competent individual is vital. The PISA adoption of global competence as a K–12 student capacity generates the challenge for educators to learn about the knowledge, attitudes, skills, values, and experiences students need during their formative years to nurture this competence (Asia Society OECD, 2018).

Global competence assessment highlights the importance of integrating real-life learning activities into schooling. OECD/PISA stresses that educators need to learn how to integrate this information into the daily classroom life every year for all students. Since PISA also assesses how well students can apply what they learn in school to real-life situations, educators must create real-life learning activities for developing competence in a globally oriented school environment (Asia Society/OECD, 2018).

The Global Learning Platform integrates competency development to target and support students' preparation as competent workers and citizens. The ISC's work connects learning to real-life activities, enabling educators, learners, and others to connect to the larger systems beyond school (Snyder, 2019; Sullivan, 2019).

UNESCO Global Citizenship

The ISC supports the UNESCO tenets that citizenship is nurtured in individuals by practicing skills in the cognitive, socio-emotional, and behavioral learning areas. The cognitive domain focuses on gaining knowledge and developing critical thinking skills. The social-emotional area nurtures the development of a learner's values, attitudes, and social skills for living with others respectfully and peacefully. The behavioral aspect is learning how to take effective, responsible action at local, national, and global levels (UNESCO, 2015; 2017).

The Global Learning Platform links the three learning domains for educating the whole individual for thinking, feeling, and acting with principled values as a lifelong, globally oriented learner. The platform integrates the UNESCO citizenship idea into the curriculum, instruction, and activities to provide the knowledge, resources, and examples for fostering the thinking, social, and action-taking capacities needed to be responsible citizens with a global worldview.

The Global Learning Benchmarks

The new professional challenge for educators is integrating global learning into the school's daily curriculum and the schoolwide culture of learning and living. The Global Learning Platform brings all the pieces from ISC, UNESCO, PISA, and OECD together for teachers and students to include practices to expand competency development. Most importantly, it stimulates new ways of thinking about becoming competent global citizens. Textbox 8.2 lists the 10 GLBs, organized into 1) The Global Learning Environment for Students and 2) Student Preparation for Success in a Global Environment (Snyder, 2019; Sullivan, 2019).

The validated benchmarks add to an educator's and a student's knowledge of a school as a globally oriented learning system for developing capable world citizens. The GLBs connect the individual, organization, and networked systems in the change process to create a holistic view of the school context. The GLBs and their five indicators help educators and students think differently about schooling (Sullivan, 2019).

The GLBs generate opportunities to excite and invigorate conversations and thinking that raise the levels of insight about the capabilities needed to be successful in our complex global society. The benchmarks served as examples for schools to reorient the learning environment. Over time, they developed more fully and were integrated into curriculum development and activities. The GLBs are a resource for including meaningful opportunities to practice relevant learning, and they also provide a school with measures to strategically set up the most effective and relevant processes for increasing each student's global competence.

TEXTBOX 8.2. ISC GLOBAL LEARNING BENCHMARKS

I. The Global Learning Environment for Students Cluster

GLB 1: The curriculum provides opportunities to learn about local and global forces that influence change.
GLB 2: The school as a growing system has a vision and a plan to connect with the global community and its dynamic forces.
GLB 3: Educators participate in professional development activity in a globally networked environment to promote learning.

GLB 4: Partnerships with local, regional, and other global businesses enhance the direction of school development.
GLB 5: The school annually shows evidence of improving or sustaining student performance levels, using multiple local, regional, or international measures.

II. Student Preparation for Success in a Global Environment Cluster

GLB 6: Current knowledge about human learning guides teaching and learning practices throughout the school.
GLB 7: International school developments or programs are included in the school's curriculum to promote global learning opportunities for all students.
GLB 8: Students are developing capacities for success in the evolving global workforce, which includes emerging technologies.
GLB 9: Students learn and use democratic decision-making processes that value diversity and promote equity and the appreciation for human life as foundations for becoming global citizens.
GLB 10: Students demonstrate an orientation for caring about the human community and its sustainable development.

THE STORY OF A GLOBAL LEARNING BENCHMARK INTEGRATION PROJECT

During 2018 and 2019, the ISC conducted a case study on the multi-year Corbett Global Learning Benchmark Integration Project (Sullivan, 2019). The study researched the hurdles and successes faced during implementation. Corbett Preparatory School of IDS (Corbett) in Tampa, Florida, a private, pre-K–8 school, was suited to globalize its program using the GLB Integration Project. Corbett had a culture of adding innovations, including the GLBs, into its practices and assessing the results. This section highlights the research findings and important steps for creating globally oriented learning systems.

An ISC-Corbett team designed the research-based project to include opportunities to gain global knowledge for orienting the learning context and developing students' global citizenship. During the project, data and anecdotal information were collected that serve as the basis for our story. Data sources included 1) a pre– and post–Global Learning Benchmark Likert administration, 2) Focus Groups, 3) Observations, and 4) Teacher Weekly Reports. It is hoped that sharing details from this experience will offer readers new insights about how to lead schools toward sustainable development from systems and complex thinking perspectives.

The co-created goals of the GLB Integration Project were to 1) use the GLBs to guide teacher expansion of knowledge for fostering students' global competence and citizenship, 2) create a schoolwide global learning orientation, and 3) build systems to foster sustainable change. The GLBs offered leaders a global lens for organizing school development to adapt to the local and global context, and they helped staff make sense of global information for decision-making to reorient the school to prepare students (Snyder, 2019; Sullivan, 2019).

Data and anecdotal information showed that the staff's attitudes about using the integration strategy changed after interactions with trainers at focus groups, workshops, or coaching sessions. Before the project, the GLBs were typically considered "add-ons" in the classroom instead of being integrated into the curriculum or activities. Some comments show the changing attitudes: "Until the workshop yesterday, we were doing what we normally do in lessons and then reflecting on how they fit with the GLBs. Now we will be intentional in our planning" (Sullivan, 2019).

The ISC team used the primary challenges to equitable living and sustainability issues listed in the UN's Sustainable Development Goals as a universal global context for its training events and programs, and through Project data analysis, it determined that teachers did not have adequate knowledge or examples to envision a global learning context. Thus, the SDGs were included in the Corbett Project to increase teachers' knowledge of a global context and to create a shared view of the school's context (Snyder, 2019; Sullivan, 2019).

In 2018, the ISC team fully integrated student competency development into the project when PISA began assessing global competence in 15-year-olds. Adding the PISA resources gave more examples and strategies to promote developing citizenship and career competencies. The ISC data analysis showed a need for more student engagement with the GLBs to create ownership for developing global citizenship.

At the project's start, the staff was in a readiness stage. During implementation, the data reported that teams were at varying GLB levels of use and integration, and more training about the GLBs, globalization, and change processes was needed. In the focus groups, a coaching dynamic emerged, which aided staff in understanding global knowledge for integrating, as it made sense for Corbett's programs. Teams shared that start-up experiences were challenging, with integration becoming easier as they learned more about global ideas. The ISC therefore determined that coaching needed to be a part of a school's development process and future projects.

The staff that frequently globalized learning and context with the GLBs reported an improved understanding of seeing the big picture made up of connected parts. Their remarks show the staff's increased systemic thinking: "GLBs are a starting point for planning, guiding us in 'how to' integrate global learning into our school and classrooms. With the GLBs, our program will be richer concerning big concepts and perspectives" (Sullivan, 2019).

In the project's implementation, the school development process evolved naturally into participants thinking about the school as a complex system for decision-making and planning for globalizing the curriculum, instruction, and activities. The staff became aware of the interconnectedness and interdependencies of the GLBs, which helped individuals understand that a system is holistic and integrated (Snyder, 2019; Sullivan, 2019).

DEVELOPING SUSTAINABLE SCHOOLING

In this last section, we explore the question: "So what does this have to do with developing schools as living systems?" The answer lies in the relationship between different levels of the school system, starting with the students and then turning to a systems approach to school development and professional development, the latter of which are the original foundations of the ISC program.

Students as Global Learners

Students today are engaging more often across national boundaries and deal with more interconnected complex societal challenges than ever before. The student exists in an entangled society in which they are "uniquely shaped by and shapers-of complex societal challenges" (Wessels, et al., 2022: p. 3). As an isolated institution, the school has disappeared, leaving a disconnect for students who live in complex social networks outside the school walls. Meeting students' needs and realities calls for schools to incorporate this external reality into the daily life of the school. Perspectives from complexity thinking with a global lens are key.

Complexity thinking helps educators recognize that relationships are the interconnections and interactions that form an entangled societal system. The entangled relationships result in entangled demands and challenges that require holistic critical thinking to see overarching issues that can impact any part of the whole unexpectantly and unknowingly. School change must occur in the context of entanglement theory because, in some way, everything is connected and impacts everything else (Wessels et al., 2022). Educators must ask strategic questions to determine how best to prepare the entangled student for future success in an entangled society.

Strategic School Development

The Global Learning Platform is combined with a strategic school development approach based on the school as a living system. In the Strategic School Development process, educators ask: "What are the possibilities? Where are we on our journey? Where do we want to be? What is our plan to get there? and How can we organize to get there?" (Sullivan, 2019).

The Global Learning Platform provides the knowledge and experiences for making informed answers to these questions. It creates a common fund of knowledge, shapes perspectives, and provides tools and resources for working together to influence change. The platform aligns with the vision of all school development decisions within the system and its parts. The elements guide strategic development toward the adaptive vision of what is possible, and the information from the relationships shapes the emergent strategic plan to determine what to maintain, delete, or innovate for change in the entangled systems (Sullivan, 2019).

The Global Learning Platform linked to strategic school development helps educators have insights about knowing "what to know" and knowing "how to do" by using "what you know." The platform enables teachers, the main change agents in schools, to understand the global challenges and opportunities faced by that the school when deciding what and how to change in preparing students. Teachers come to understand that there is a relationship between the school development process and emergent strategic change.

A person's role in each level of entangled systems is symbiotic. Each system shapes the other, and the systems shape the person. The strategic questions help educators make sense of systems and their entanglements to guide the direction of change management. The potential of the system, its networks, and the individual is explored to determine the most effective ways to influence change toward an envisioned future, which also can evolve with the times. Effective and efficient change management occurs by identifying if the system under consideration is simple, complicated, complex, or chaotic in order to select the suitable strategy for that system.

Complex systems require a shift in how one thinks and acts to facilitate change because they are unpredictable, relational, and non-linear. The emergence of opportunities and new challenges is dynamic in strategic planning and intervention selection in complex and chaotic systems (Snyder et al., 2000/2008; Redman & Wiek, 2021). Complexity thinking empowers one to critically analyze problems from various views for multiple solutions to reach the tipping point for change. The ISC's Complexity Thinking as a Way of Living provides coherence and clarity for thinking about change management.

Professional Development for Building Sustainable Schooling

The ISC's professional development system focuses on "What needs to be learned," "Why it needs to be learned," "How it is best learned," and "How do you use it to facilitate change?" (Fitzgerald & Sullivan, 2023). ISC training supports UNESCO Priority Action Area 3 to build educators' capacities to be learners with the skills, knowledge, values, and attitudes to be global citizens. Educators must go through the same self-directed learning and reflection cycle as students to gain knowledge and capacities for acquiring a global worldview (UNESCO, 2021). What teachers learn is the same as what students need to learn to be global citizens. The focus is on learning, not teaching.

The ISC Global Platform guides professional development activities' context, content, and learning process. Because the platform is a complex system, it gives staff a holistic view of what is needed to become globally oriented learners and citizens. It provides the knowledge, models, and examples to expand capabilities. Educators gain the knowledge to learn ways to adapt to local and global contexts to provide the best possible schooling.

The ISC's training focuses on understanding and applying change management based on systems and complexity principles processes for school development. Educators, the change agents, use systems and complexity thinking to understand systems and context to choose strategies to facilitate change. Training includes opportunities to develop a complexity-thinking mindset to use systems analysis and tools to make informed, purposeful action. The training uses the view that a school is a living system that stresses connectedness, which emphasizes transforming *how people work together* (Wheatley, 2017).

A CALL TO ACTION

The ISC's Call to Action is for educators to prepare students as complexity thinkers with a global worldview to address the challenging demands of society, the economy, and the environment. Educators are encouraged to gain insights and knowledge from the ISC's story, research, and the Global Learning Platform to provide relevant learning. Schools need to make the development of an individual's capacity to think critically to address complex issues in complex systems a priority. Educators are invited to use the

Complexity Thinking as a Way of Living mindset to reimagine schooling for increasingly complex times.

Educators are also asked to learn how to reorient schooling to a global perspective, and to use an emergent strategic development plan for whole-school change. The school community is encouraged to use the ISC story for inspiration to make the best choices for preparing their students individually and collectively to address the pervasive, complex demands and challenges of our global society, economy, and planet's sustainability.

REFERENCES

Asia Society/OECD. (2018). *Teaching for global competence in a rapidly changing world*. OECD & Asia Society: Paris, New York. https://doi.org/10.1787/9789264289024-en

Bokova, I. (10 Nov. 2014). Opening speech of the World Conference on Education for Sustainable Development (ESD) in Aichi-Nagoya, Japan. *UN News: Global perspective human stories*. https://news.un.org/en/story/2014/11/483212

Brown, Shae L. (2019). A patterning approach to complexity thinking and understanding for students: A case study. *Northeast Journal of Complex Systems*, 1(1), Article 6. DOI: 10.22191/nejcs/vol1/iss1/6

Brundtland, G. H. (1987). *Our common future: Report of the World Commission on Environment and Development*. Geneva, UN-Dokument A/42/427. http://www.un-documents.net/ocf-ov.htm

Capra, F., & Luisi, P. (2014). *The systems view of life: A unifying vision*. Cambridge: Cambridge University Press.

Fitzgerald, J., & Sullivan, E. (2023). Toward the school as a sustainable global learning center system. In K. J. Snyder & K. M. Snyder (Eds.), *Systems thinking for sustainable schooling: A mindshift for educators to lead and achieve quality in schools*. Lanham, MD: Rowman & Littlefield Publishers.

Harmat, L., & Herbert, A. (2020). Complexity thinking as a tool to understand the Didactics of Psychology. *Frontier in Psychology*, 11. Article 542446. doi:10.3389/fpsyg.2020.542446

Merali, Y., & Allen, P. (2011). Complexity and systems thinking. In S. Maguire, P. Allen, and B. McKelvey (Eds.), *The Sage Handbook of Complexity and Management*. SAGE.

Organization for Economic Co-operation and Development (OECD). (2018). *PISA 2018 global competence*. www.oecd.org/pisa/pisa-2018-global-competence.htm

Piacentini, M., Barrett, M., Boix Mansilla, V., Deardorff, D., & Lee, H. W. (2017). *Preparing our youth for an inclusive and sustainable world: The OECD PISA global competence framework*. Paris: OECD. https://www.oecd.org/education/Global-competency-for-an-inclusive-world.pdf

Redman, A., & Wiek, A. (2021). Competencies for advancing transformations towards sustainability. *Frontiers in Education*. www.frontiersin.org/articles/10.3389/feduc.2021.785163.

Rieckmann, M. (2018). Learning to transform the world: Key competencies in education for sustainable development. In A. Leicht, J. Heiss, & W. Byun (Eds.), *Issues and trends in education for sustainable development* (pp. 39–59). https://unesdoc.unesco.org/ark:/48223/pf0000261802

Snowden, D. (2020). *Weaving sense-making into the fabric of our world.* Cognitive Edge - The Cynefin Company.

Snyder, K. (2019). Preparing globally competent students: The k-12 schooling challenge. 2019 Global Conference on Education and Research Proceedings Book, ID 257.

Snyder, K. J., Acker-Hocevar, M., & Snyder, K. M. (2000, 2008). *Living on the edge of chaos: Leading schools into the global age.* ASQ: The Quality Press.

Sullivan, E. (2019). *The ISC global learning benchmark integration school development at Corbett Prep: A case study.* 2019 Global Conference on Education and Research Proceedings Book, ID 257.

Teixeira de Melo, A. (2020). *Performing complexity: Building foundations for the practice of complex thinking.* 10.1007/978-3-030-46245-1

UNESCO. (2015). *Global citizenship education: Topics and learning objectives.* Paris: UNESCO. https://unesdoc.unesco.org/ark:/48223/pf0000232993

UNESCO. (2017). *Education for sustainable development goals: Learning objectives.* Paris: UNESCO. https://unesdoc.unesco.org/ark:/48223/pf0000247444

UNESCO. (2020). *Education for sustainable development: A roadmap.* Paris: UNESCO.https://unesdoc.unesco.org/ark:/48223/pf0000374802

UNESCO. (2021). *Reimagining our futures together: A new social contract for education.* Paris: UNESCO. https://unesdoc.unesco.org/ark:/48223/pf0000379381

United Nations Academic Impact. (n.d.). *Global citizenship.* https://www.un.org/en/academic-impact/global-citizenship

United Nations Department of Economic and Social Affairs. (n.d.). *Do you know all the 17 Goals?* http://sdgs.un.org/goals

Wessels, K., Bakker, C., Wals, A., & Lengkeek, G. (2022). Rethinking pedagogy in the face of complex societal challenges: Helpful perspectives for teaching the entangled student. *Pedagogy, Culture & Society.* DOI: 10.1080/14681366.2022.2108125

Wheatley, M. (2017). Whom *do we choose to be*? Oakland, CA: Berrett-Koehler.

Chapter 9

Storytelling as a Strategic Leadership Tool

Kristen M. Snyder

The culture of a school is recognized as one of the key ingredients to achieving sustainable quality, yet it is one of the least understood phenomena among leaders. Organizational culture is abstract, difficult to observe, and certainly challenging to develop. Defining organizational culture is even more obscure for the majority who grasp to explain the unknown. Arts-based practices, such as storytelling, can help leaders understand and shape the organization's culture.

Storytelling has been a powerful tool for centuries used in different cultures to share history and experiences. Stories enable us to communicate ideas that go beyond the rational and structural; they help us to imagine and represent the difficult. As a co-creative process, storytelling builds cultures of engagement naturally through the shared context and sense of shared meaning that results.

As a leadership tool, stories can be used to communicate ideas, norms, and values, and to facilitate unlearning, which is necessary to create space for developing cultures of innovation and continuous improvement. Stories can help to frame and re-frame information, making them a valuable tool for development, transformation, and innovation. Leaders who use storytelling successfully recognize the impact it has on creating an organization that is participatory, resilient, reflective, flexible, and innovative.

The purpose of this chapter is to present and illustrate the use of storytelling as a leadership tool to develop work cultures in schools built on trust, courage, and dialogue to support sustainable quality in education. In the first part of this chapter, readers will develop an understanding of what is organizational culture and how it can be developed to support the systems of work to foster sustainable quality development in schools.

In the second part of the chapter, storytelling as a contemporary arts-based practice will be presented as a co-creative process to build cultures of engagement that are supported by a systems view of schooling. In the third section, two approaches to storytelling will be described to provide the reader with easy access to begin applying storytelling in schools. Practical examples as well will be offered to illustrate how storytelling can be used as a tool to identify and shape the school's culture.

THE CULTURAL WEB OF SCHOOLING: A HISTORICAL PERSPECTIVE

Schools are traditionally challenged to renovate, reconstruct, and/or innovate the learning environment. Such challenges are stimulated by educational policy, nationally and internationally, that prescribe an agenda for reform. Policy initiatives from the last two decades underscore the need for schools to prepare youth with twenty-first--century skills, including digital literacy, creative thinking, teamwork (Abbey, 2008), cultural sensitivity, and sustainable development (OECD, 2018). Meeting these challenges requires innovation and the redesign of schooling around the world (Snyder & Snyder, 2021).

While there are examples of innovation (Fischer et al., 2020), most research indicates that innovation is short-lived or never achieved at a level of sustainability, calling for us to rethink education (Sterling, 2010). Reasons given include a lack of leadership (Snyder, 2008), a lack of a systems orientation, and a disconnect between the cultural values and behaviors with the mission and goals of the school (Cuban, 2013). Consequently, small projects remain just that: small and short-lived.

Wolf and Brennen (2014) suggest that an "innovation-supportive culture is important for both the generation and implementation of innovations" (p. 3) at the organizational level. Organizational innovation reflects a system-wide change that includes a shift in the work processes and structures designed to deliver value to all stakeholders. Building organizational cultures based on teamwork, autonomy, risk-taking, support for change, and trust (Snyder & Snyder, 2021; Wolf & Brennen, 2014) are necessary components to support sustainable innovation at the organizational level.

Getting innovative in schools is no easy task. As Cuban (2012) points out, policy change is not enough for innovation in education to occur. Contradictions and places of resistance need to be understood to develop the kinds of work cultures needed to promote growth and sustainable development. Sarason (1996) claims that leaders often are gatekeepers of change, making decisions for teachers. Using innovation as a driver for quality will require that leaders release the hold on culture and create structures for engagement, shared decision-making, and teaming in order to foster spaces for co-creation.

Sullivan (2023) demonstrates the important connections between organizational culture and innovation in her work with quantum leadership. Sustaining quality in schools, she contends, requires that leaders build cultures of engagement based on communication and dialogue to socially construct shared meaning and direction. Quantum leaders use strategic conversations to encourage commitment, build community, and develop a shared language that informs the strategic plan and creates knowledge for change. Creating space to tell stories helps to translate ideas into action.

Snyder et al. (2018) found that many leaders struggle to understand how to balance structure with culture to create the conditions necessary to sustain quality development in an age of complexity. All too often, the focus is on structure and policy, ignoring the power and importance of people, values, and behaviors as key ingredients for sustainable organizational development. They also found that leaders who understand the importance of connecting structure and culture have stronger internal systems that are adaptive and responsive to change, and thus more sustainable.

Researchers in quality management reinforce this finding and the need to connect culture and structure to foster trust and courage for innovation. Dahlgaard and Dahlgaard-Park (2003) contend that achieving and sustaining quality in any organization is dependent upon the integration of the 4 Ps: people, process, products, and partnership. Their models reflect the interdependence of these four components to generate innovation and organizational learning. Creating conditions for cultures of engagement to support collaborative innovation is imperative for sustainable development.

ORGANIZATIONAL CULTURE

Organizational culture reflects the systems and structures through which people give meaning to organizational life (Schein, 2009). Culture is known as the way we do things in a context and is broadly defined as "a shared and learned world of experiences, meanings, values and understandings which inform people, and are expressed, reproduced, and communicated partly in the symbolic form" (Alvesson, 2002: p. 3).

Culture manifests itself in language, stories, and symbols that are used to communicate the values and purpose of the organization (Schein, 2009). Further, it is reinforced by the design and structure of the organization and the systems and procedures of work. Quality cultures are determined by the way in which the language, stories, and symbols reinforce the strategies and work processes of the organization. Where there is an alignment of the two, sustainable quality development is supported.

One of the cornerstones of organizational culture is communication, which takes place in many forms. It is through communication that meaning is created through a collective act. Bantz (1993) states that "organizational communication is the collective creation, maintenance, and transformation of organizational meaning and organizational expectations through the sending and using of messages" (p. 18). Weick (1995) calls this "sensemaking" through enactment. He suggests that people in an organization participate in shaping their environment. The actions they take help to give rise to structures and meaning.

Schein (2009) defines culture as "a pattern of shared tacit assumptions that was learned by a group as it solves its problems of external adaption and internal integration" (p. 27). When the patterns demonstrate the successful resolution of problems, the tacit assumptions are shared with other members and reinforced by the way members perceive, think, and feel about the problems. According to Schein, there are three levels of culture that exist within organizations: artifacts, espoused values, and underlying assumptions.

The first level reflects "artifacts," which can be observed on the surface, for example, language, products, stories about the company, and organization charts. These can be easily discerned but are hard to decipher. Underlying the artifacts, on the second level, are "espoused values," for example, strategies, goals, and philosophies. They often leave large areas of behavior unexplained, and to get a deeper understanding, you must become aware of the "underlying assumptions," which are the third level of organizational culture. These assumptions are unconscious and taken for granted, and as such, they tend to be very hard to change.

Grasping and being able to identify the complex nature of the school's culture is a critical first step to building sustainable quality in education. When leaders fail to understand the culture and its power for transformation, they blindly invite countercultures to build, which can sabotage innovation. As Martin (1992) points out, countercultures can be devastating for sustaining quality. Moreover, leaders can develop knowledge for understanding what creates different cultures to foster what is needed in the school to support innovation and engagement.

Martin (1992) identifies three main types of organizational culture: *Integrated, fragmented,* and *differentiated.* An integrated culture is characterized by a shared language, symbols, and stories that support the work of the organization to achieve its vision and goals and meet customer needs. A fragmented culture is reflected by subcultures that emerge informally, each of which has its own codes of conduct, behaviors, and language. They are typically short-lived and don't develop new norms and behaviors.

The differentiated organization is comprised of subcultures that are developed with the intent to create resistance in the organization. Differentiated cultures have their own value systems and norms, which are not in line with the vision and mission of the organization. Her framework for identifying organizational culture provides insights into the interdependence of behavior, language, attitude, values, vision, and goals of the organization.

Organizational culture is critical for leading and sustaining quality development in any organization, which today requires a new kind of culture and structure that facilitates engagement, networking, shared decision-making, and value cocreation around broader societal needs (Fundin et al., 2021). Cultures in which the values of the organization are clearly articulated and supported by interdependence of work systems provide both structure and freedom for improvisation (Snyder & Snyder, 2021). Short of this, achieving quality will be short-lived.

DEVELOPING ORGANIZATIONAL CULTURE THROUGH ARTS-BASED PRACTICES

Building organizational culture takes time and requires leaders to understand how to build systems of communication that support shared values and a collective vision. Snyder et al. (2008) suggest that culture needs to be understood as a dynamic living system that changes in response to internal and external influences. Managing this dynamic is the job of leaders, which requires that they understand how meaning is shaped in the organization and how behaviors and language reinforce values. Toward this end, there is a growing interest in arts-based practices to identify and frame the culture of an organization. Such practices include design thinking, appreciative inquiry, and storytelling. In this chapter, storytelling is explored.

Arts-based initiatives (ABI) can be powerful tools to help people to think outside the box and stimulate value co-creation (Carlucci & Schiuma, 2018). ABI engages people in aesthetic experiences through which they co-create value in their work environment, processes, and products. The movement grew from a recognition that innovation through the arts fosters a process of developing solutions to problems through a systematic iterative method that invites exploration and exploitation of new ideas (Taylor & Ladkin, 2009).

In organizations, work is often centered around concrete structures and processes that are tangible, observable, and easy to talk about. Meanwhile, the unseen dimensions of work found in the values, norms, and behaviors of organizational culture are left untouched since they are too abstract to identify. The arts make visible these unseen dimensions in a unique way, providing workers with experiences and skills to identify and reflect upon the deeper dynamics of organizational life that impact their well-being and work processes.

Arts-based experiences create an environment that frees workers from traditional ways of seeing and working by moving them out of their comfort zone, creating space for reflection, and making the invisible visible (Carlucci & Schiuma, 2018). As a co-creative process, arts-based practice stimulates out-of-the-box thinking (Rill, 2016) and helps people develop a shared understanding and common values, as well as increase creativity and innovation to promote a more productive workplace culture.

Among the arts-based practices used by many organizations and researchers today is storytelling. In the next section of this chapter, storytelling is presented as a leadership tool to identify, understand, and develop organizational cultures to create the conditions necessary for sustainable quality in education.

STORYTELLING AND ORGANIZATIONAL CULTURE

We live the stories we tell. Through our words, pictures, films, and other forms of expression, we communicate ideas and experiences that shape us and give rise to our identity. Pearce (1989) suggests that as human beings, we are storytellers who engage in the act of storytelling as a form of co-constructive communication. People do not just exchange messages but act into the actions of the other and in so doing create shared meaning and shared existence. Stories are what makes us human: we are our narratives (Hendry, 2007).

Storytelling has been a powerful tool for centuries used in different cultures to share history and experiences. Much of childhood is spent hearing myths and legends from which we build a sense of understanding about ourselves and the world to which we belong. It is through stories that children develop a sense of belief and a value system at an early age. Stories enable us to communicate ideas that go beyond the rational and structural; they help us to imagine and represent the difficult.

Stories also help to identify the values in an organization's culture (Martin, 1992; Meyer, 1995). The narratives that are shared both reflect values and reinforce them in behaviors. Meyer suggests that stories "serve to encapsulate and entrench the values which are key to an organization's culture (1995: 210). Meyer also reports on studies showing that managers who expected survey data to generate the most valuable information instead found stories to be more revealing and sparked greater dialogue and suggestions for change.

Storytelling is a social process through which we give shape to our world and identity. How we tell a story, the words we choose, as well as the angle, have a deep connection to what and how we experience our stories. By giving an account of an event, we can see relationships between events and actors and experience the experience. We can remain open to exploring rather than close off in a place of judgment. It is a dialogical, co-constructive process that fosters co-creation and shared meaning.

The dialogical model of storytelling (Snyder & Cooper, 2015) is particularly appropriate for organizations. Unlike the monologic model in which the story being shared is already complete, the dialogic form of storytelling emerges over time through co-creation. It often lacks a clear start, and it does not have a clear middle and end. The collective story unfolds over time as the multiple storytellers engage in the act of sharing their own stories based on experiences. It is this co-creative, dialogic approach to storytelling that makes it useful as a tool and process for shaping organizational cultures through participation and engagement.

STORYTELLING AS A LEADERSHIP TOOL

Stories can be used by leaders to achieve many goals (Morgan & Dennehy, 1997). For example, stories enhance recall, retention, and comprehension. They serve as well to trigger emotion, inspire, instruct, and entertain. This multifaceted strength makes storytelling an effective coaching tool for leaders (Ann & Carr, 2011) who want to shape cultures of engagement and innovation.

- Stories make complex situations and phenomena accessible.
- Stories reveal values and principles hidden in culture from the naked eye.
- Stories make visible driving forces for change that are not easy to identify.
- Stories provide a platform for understanding different perspectives.

Ann and Carr demonstrated how the construction, reconstruction, and circulation of stories in an organization make stories themselves "active players" in co-creation. As active players, stories took on a transformational role through which organizational members articulate purpose and action in their decisions and behaviors. By telling stories about the past, present, and future, leaders and members identify what was, what is, and what is desired.

As a leadership tool, stories have been used to communicate ideas, norms, and values through which culture is shaped. Storytelling has been used as well to share tacit knowledge and facilitate unlearning, which is necessary to create space for change and generate emotional connections (Sole & Wilson, 2002). Stories can be used to frame and re-frame information, making them valuable as a tool for development, transformation, and innovation.

According to Martin (1992), understanding the language and stories present in a group is important to understanding culture. She found that stories promote, approve, and disapprove of certain behaviors. Stories reveal what is important, and they "reaffirm identity and values and confirm the individual's identity with, and commitment to, the group" (Foster et al., 1998), making stories an important co-creative tool. It is thus critical for each of us as individuals and members of the community to have a platform to tell our own stories and not live by the stories that others tell of us.

Auvinen et al. (2013) found that leaders used stories in a variety of ways to motivate, inspire, prevent conflicts, influence, discover, and build trust. Sole and Wilson (2002) found in their review of the literature that stories are useful in a variety of situations: 1) to "kick-start" a new idea; 2) to socialize new members; 3) to mend relationships; and 4) to share wisdom. In the context of most organizations on any given day, the need to address each one of these situations is likely to exist. The key, however, is to know how to use storytelling to create a culture of shared engagement and innovation.

Auvinen et al. (2013) further suggest that stories can be used as a co-creative process to foster equality and break down the hierarchical barriers that are familiar in many organizations. They write, "leaders and followers are able to tell that they share the same organizational reality rather than begin trapped behind barriers arising from the hierarchical levels and differences of power in the organization" (p. 497).

As a co-creative process, storytelling builds cultures of trust through shared context and shared meaning. Auvinen et al. (ibid.) found that leaders who use storytelling successfully recognize the importance of being dyadic and the need to listen to the stories around them. More often, stories told by leaders were stimulated as a response to an employee's story. They were often not planned, but rather spontaneous, responsive, and co-creative.

TWO EXAMPLES

Two examples of stories from school development projects are offered: *"the fence"* and *"the doors are closed, but the school is open."* These stories illustrate how educators can work with organizational culture to foster conditions for achieving the goals of the school. The stories contain elements of guiding principles and values that drove decision-making and accompanying behaviors that either supported or hindered the educator's ability to provide quality for students, teachers, and parents.

Example 1: *"The building is closed, but we are open for learning"*

During the pandemic, a school in Florida in the United States used the power of culture and communication to redesign their school. They developed a hashtag: #ONECOMMUNITY and a motto: *The building is closed, but we are open for learning.* The rhetoric was carefully constructed to reflect the school's guiding principles: connection, openness, caring, and learning.

Over the course of the year, school leaders witnessed how the attitudes and behaviors of the teachers, parents, and community became shaped by this message to support their remote learning program. Parents were engaged in dialogue daily and served as a bridge to help ensure students' well-being through remote learning reinforcing the #onecommunity.

To keep connections strong with remote learners and boost morale, teachers designed small events such as "Operation curbside pick-me-up" to stay connected. They drove to student homes in cars decorated with banners that said "We love you" and greeted the remote students at their doorsteps, giving them "high-fives," safely, with the help of a wooden hand. Their behaviors and attitudes reflected the core values of keeping everyone happy, healthy, and engaged in learning during the pandemic. Their work processes were supported by the culture.

Example 2: The "fence"

Teachers in a preschool in Sweden were working hard to develop a strong relationship with parents. The school, which was in a community of diversity, struggled with issues of communication; both in written and spoken language as well as culture. Over the course of a year, they tried in numerous ways to invite the parents to be a part of the school community: lunches, picnics, open houses, anything that would engage the parents.

Frustrated, they decided to conduct a cultural analysis of their school, which is when they began to see the core of the problem. The school was situated in an area of high crime, and as such, they had a fence surrounding the school. To enter, one needed to open the gate, which had a sign hanging on it: "Please leave your child here." As part of the cultural analysis, they began to observe the behavioral patterns of parents, teachers, and students and paid closer attention to the written forms of communication.

What they saw was eye-opening: the parents arrived on time. As they approached the gate, they would "hand over" their child to the teachers, often without opening the gate. The fence, accompanied by the sign "leave your child here," was interpreted by the parents as a border they should not pass.

Soon the teachers began to understand how their acts of care had been reinterpreted by other cultural experiences of bordering.

The sign on the gate was changed, and parents began to see the value of the fence as caring for the safety of their children. It didn't take long for new behaviors to develop. Relations between the parents and teachers grew strong. Parents began attending school events, and parent-teacher dialogues became common. The lines of communication opened, and parents began to contact teachers with questions or ideas that they had; a culture of engagement and trust was formed.

APPLYING STORYTELLING IN YOUR SCHOOL

Developing skills in the art of storytelling in organizations is not complicated. It takes time, but it is much more within our reach than first meets the eye. Stories are all around us; they are within us. Stories are information in context. When listening to what is being said around us, we begin to engage in the storytelling process. Developing skills in storytelling requires that one develop a sense of listening to the words around us; the ideas shared; who is sharing them; how they are being shared; and the kinds of information that is omitted.

Each school has a social culture that is comprised of symbols, roles, relationships, norms, and values, which are communicated in a variety of ways. Understanding the culture can be done by identifying and examining information in the form of messages, metaphors, symbols, pictures, or group membership. Together, these pieces of information become parts of the broader story of the school that reflect the values, norms, and behaviors.

Many approaches to storytelling exist. In this chapter, two are presented for their application to education. The first approach is based on the concept of listening to the words around you, using the Gemba walking process from quality management theory. The second approach is a systemic model for moving the organization from individual stories to collective stories. In this model, the focus is given to participatory practice and the cocreation of the school's story. Both are useful and can be combined.

STORYTELLING THROUGH "LISTENING IN" DURING GEMBA WALKING

Gemba walking is a process and tool used in quality management. Each day, leaders walk the floor of their production facilities and listen to the workers on the front line about what is happening. It is a form of quality management based on the notion that persons closest to the work are the most knowledgeable. Through Gemba Walking and listening to the stories of their workers, leaders gain a sense of where the production is effective and where small improvements need to be made to ensure continuous high quality.

The concept of Gemba Walking translates nicely to the context of schooling and can be used by leaders to listen to the stories around them. Educators are naturally engaged daily in the work of the school. As you visit the classrooms, walk through the hallways, participate in staff meetings, or listen to comments from parents and kids about the school, important insights are embedded in the words shared and the behaviors observed. Paying attention to this kind of information and acknowledging them through dialogue can become the drivers through which to identify areas of strength and weakness.

Begin to identify the culture that is dominant in your school by reflecting upon and observing behaviors, language, and attitudes. What is the tone of the language you hear? Is it positive? Does it reflect frustration? Does it reflect values such as respect, openness, curiosity, segregation, isolation, and power? What kind of energy do you feel in your school? Is the same energy shared by all members, or is it different among people? Does your organization have informal subteams, or do you work openly and transparently? How do you feel and react to the kinds of words, behaviors, and attitudes that exist in your group? Are they what you need to work together as a cohesive school, or do you need to develop some new behaviors and shared language to help you become more effective?

As a school team, use the following questions to begin a reflection and dialogue in your school to understand and develop the kind of school culture that best fits your needs. Consider both the stories, language, values, and behaviors. Of importance is to develop stories and behaviors that will help your school to become responsive and adaptable to the needs of students, parents, and policy.

Stories:

1. How do you describe and talk about your school? What are the stories you tell? What are the kinds of words you use to describe who you are, what you do, and why you exist as a school?
2. How do others talk about your school? What are the stories they tell? What are the kinds of words they use to describe who you are, what you do, and why you exist as a school?
3. What story do you want to tell about your school in 1 year? 2 years?

Culture: Values, Behaviors

1. What behaviors are important to you in a school?

2. What values are important to your school to create sustainable quality cultures?
3. What behaviors exist among your school's team that are important to keep?
4. What words are important to reflect the school's guiding principles and values?

STORYTELLING MODEL FOR SCHOOL DEVELOPMENT

The second approach to storytelling for school development is a systems-oriented process in which all members of the school (staff, board, etc.) are engaged to develop a collective story for the school. The intent is

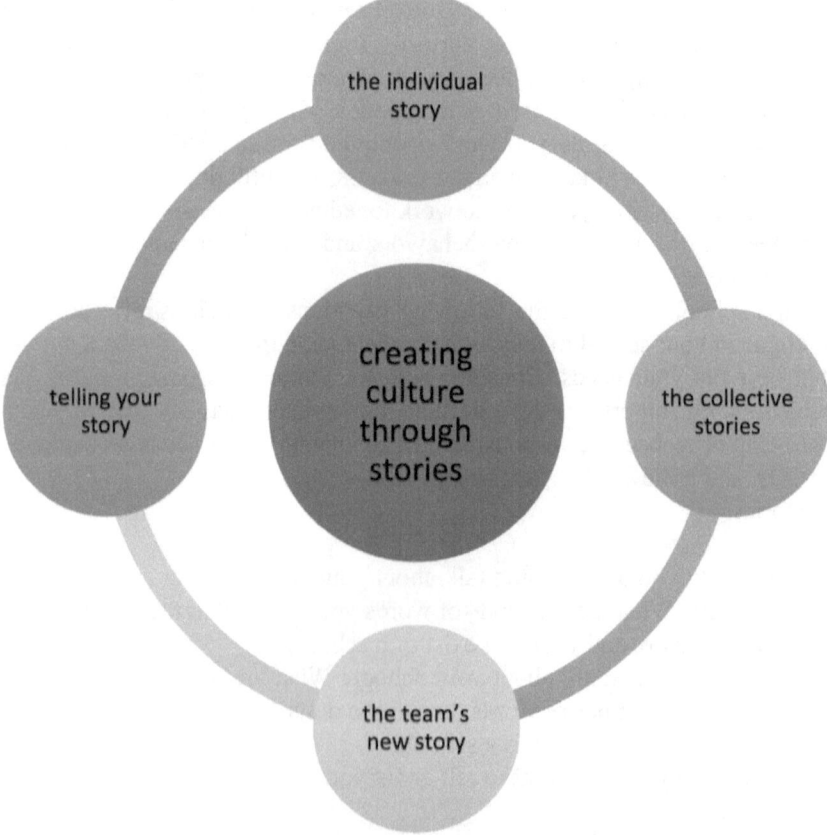

Figure 9.1. The organizational storytelling process

to align the language and story of the school with the work processes, goals, vision and mission, and behaviors and attitudes.

Step 1: The Individual Story: The process begins with the individual story. Each person reflects on what they perceive to be characteristics of the school, including its strengths and weakness. They can tell their story from the perspective of a teacher, a student, or a parent to express how they would describe the school. The story can begin with keywords or an event of something that took place that reflects the school's essence.

Step 2: The Collective Stories: To move from the individual to the collective you will want to create an architecture in the school for dialogue and reflection. It can be a temporary meeting space or a regular forum for sharing and dialogue. In this venue, each person should share their story with the group. Members should listen actively to identify strengths in the individual stories.

As part of the collective process, record the key factors identified and dialogue about their importance for the school. In what ways do they connect to and support the goals, vision, and guiding principles of the school? Are the stories reinforced by behaviors and attitudes?

Some of which you may want to keep and others you may use to identify areas of needed improvement.

Step 3: The Team/School Story: When you have listened to the individual stories from the group, and perhaps even from parents and students, it is now time to connect the stories to the goals, vision, and mission of the school. During this process, it can be useful to have access to any written documents you have about the school: school plan, protocols, expectations, etc. Include as well any symbol systems that may be present: the layout of the school, the interior design, the art on the walls, and any metaphors, formal or informal, that are used regularly.

As a group, examine the different pieces of information and dialogue about what stories you want to share. What stories do you hope to hear from parents? From the media? From current students and past students? From other schools? What behaviors are important to support your stories?

Step 4: Telling Your School's Story: Stories can be communicated in a myriad of ways: verbally, visually, through music, media, and other art forms. Technology today affords a wealth of opportunities to communicate your school's story. It also creates opportunities for counter-stories to be heard. It is thus important to be aware of both the kinds of stories, as well as who and how the stories are being shared.

In school, stories are reinforced by signs and symbols. In media, stories are reinforced through posts on social media and short films, among others. Keep in mind that stories are both verbal and visual. The words that are included in formal documents should match with the guiding principles and the behaviors of staff to foster the kind of culture desired.

A CALL TO ACTION

This chapter aims to provide educators with an understanding of organizational culture and its role in fostering the conditions for sustaining quality in education. Storytelling has been presented as a concrete tool that leaders can use to both identify and shape the kind of culture that will help the school innovate and sustain quality in response to the changing needs of students and society.

For many, the concept of arts-based practice and storytelling as a leadership tool may seem like a far stretch from the realities of life in schools today. However, it is closer than one might think; stories are embedded within our cultural and historical ways of talking and sharing. We are storytellers when we share our experiences with others and listen to a friend or colleague talk about their day. These are the stories that make up our daily lives. The purpose of this chapter is to frame the natural aspects of storytelling as a process and skill to help leaders strengthen cultures of commitment and engagement in schools.

Using storytelling to develop work cultures that foster sustainable quality development implies that the stories reflect the kinds of behaviors, norms, and values the school espouses. If the stories, over time, are not in line with the vision and goals of the school, a culture of differentiation will form and become destructive. If the school already has a strong culture of teamwork, clearly articulated goals, and an established culture of trust, then the storytelling process may advance more clearly from the individual stories to the collective vision more quickly.

Storytelling and arts-based practices provide the balance between structure, co-creation, and improvization that bridges the right side and left side of the brain. Storytelling can become the organizational mechanism through which schools can foster a new mindset to balance the bureaucratic structures and accountability demands with creativity and innovation for sustainable quality in schools.

It is the hope of this author that you are inspired to listen to the stories within yourself and around you amongst your colleagues. What are those stories, and what do they say about the culture of your school? What story do you want your school to be known for? Tell your story and live the stories you tell.

REFERENCES

Abbey, N. (2008). *Developing 21st-century teaching and learning: Dialogic literacy.* New Horizons for Learning.

Alvesson, M. (2002). *Understanding organizational culture.* SAGE.

Carr, A. N. (2011). Inside outside leadership development: coaching and storytelling potential. *Journal of Management Development,* 30(3), 297–310.

Auvinen, T. Aaltio, I., & Blomqvist, K. (2013). Constructing leadership by storytelling: the meaning of trust and narratives. *Leadership & Organizational Development Journal,* 34(6), 496–514.

Bantz, C. R. (1993). *Understanding organisations: Interpreting organisational communication culture.* University of South Carolina Press.

Carlucci, D., & Schiuma, G. (2018). The power of the arts in business. *Journal of Business Research,* 85, 342–347.

Cuban, L. (2013). Why so many structural changes in schools and so little reform in teaching practice? *Journal of Educational Administration,* 51(2), 109–125.

Park-Dahlgaard, S. M., & Dahlgaard, J. (2003). Human dimension: critical to sustainable quality development. In T. Conti, Y. Kondo, & G. Watson (Eds.), *Quality into the 21st Century: Perspectives on Quality, Competitiveness & Sustained Performance.* ASQ: A Quality Press.

Fischer, G. Lundin, J., & Lindberg, O. J. (2020). Rethinking and reinventing learning, education and collaboration in the digital age: from creating technologies to transforming cultures. *International Journal of Information and Learning Technology,* 37(5), 241–252.

Foster, N., Cebis, M., Majteles, S., Mathur, A., Morgan, R., Preuss, J., Tiwari, V., & Wilkinson, D. (1998). The role of story-telling in organizational leadership. *Leadership & Organization Development Journal,* 20(1), 11–17.

Fundin, A., Backström, T., & Johansson, P. E. (2021). Exploring the emergent quality management paradigm. *Total Quality Management & Business Excellence,* 32(5–6), 476–488.

Hendry, P. M. (2007). The future of narrative. *Qualitative Inquiry,* 13(4), 487–498.

Martin, J. (1992). *Cultures in organizations: Three perspectives.* Oxford University Press.

Meyer, J. C. (1995). Tell me a story: eliciting organizational values from narratives. *Communication quarterly,* 43(2), 210–224.

Morgan, S., & Dennehy, R. F. (1997). The power of organizational storytelling: a management development perspective. *Journal of Management Development,* 16(7), 494–501.

Organization for Economic Co-operation and Development [OECD]. (2018). *2018 PISA.* Retrieved from www.oecd.org/pisa

Pearce, W. B. (1989). *Communication and the human condition.* Southern Illinois University Press.

Rill, B. (2016). Resonant co-creation as an approach to strategic innovation. *Journal of Organizational Change Management,* 29(7), 1135–1152.

Schein, E. H. (2009). *The corporate culture survival guide.* Jossey-Bass.

Sarason, S. (1996). Revisiting the culture of the school and the problem of change. Teachers College Press.

Snyder, K. J., & Snyder, K. M. (2021). Building sustainable systems for schooling in turbulent times: Big ideas from the sciences. In Jeffrey Glanz (Ed.), *Crisis and Pandemic Leadership: Implications for meeting the needs of students, teachers and parents.* Rowman & Littlefield.

Snyder, K., Ingelsson, P., & Bäckström, I. (2018). Using design thinking to support value-based leadership for sustainable quality development. *Business Process Management Journal*, 24(6), 1289–1301.

Snyder, K., & Cooper, K. (2015). Innovating schools through dialogic arts-based practice: Ingredients for engaging students with a whole new mind. *Journal for Learning through the Arts*, 11(1), 1–20.

Snyder, K. J., Acker-Hocever, M., & Snyder, K. M. (2008). *Living on the edge of chaos: Leading schools into the global age.* ASQ: A Quality Press.

Sole, D., & Wilson, D. G. (2002). *Storytelling in organizations: The power and traps of using stories to share knowledge in organizations.* LILA: Harvard Graduation School of Education.

Sterling, S. (2010). *Living in the earth: Towards and education of our times.* SAGE.

Sullivan, E. (2023). The quantum school leader as a strategic systems thinker. In K. J. Snyder & K. M. Snyder (Eds.), *Systems thinking for sustainable schooling: A mindshift for educators to lead and achieve quality schools.* Lanham, MD: Rowman & Littlefield.

Taylor, S. S., & Ladkin, D. (2009). Understanding arts-based methods in managerial development. *Academy of Management Learning & Education*, 8(1), 55–69.

Weick, K. (1995). *Sensemaking in organizations.* SAGE.

Wolf, F., & Brennan, L. (2014). Framing the impact of organizational culture on innovation. 10.13140/2.1.2416.0004

About the Editors and Contributors

Kristen M. Snyder, PhD is Professor in Quality Management and Associate Professor in Education at Mid Sweden University. Over the decades, Snyder has contributed to research and development in education, with a focus on quality and leadership development. Through her roles as Director of Research for the International School Connection, Inc. (1999–2010) and Research Director for the Center for School and Quality Development (2001–2004) at Mid Sweden University, she also developed two benchmark systems for quality in education. Additionally, she led the international validation studies of the School Work Culture Profile (SCWP) Instrument in Hungary, Russia, Spain, and Sweden. Currently, the SWCP is used in the national Principal Certification program in Sweden. She is the author of numerous publications on leadership and innovation in schools. Her work is grounded in a systems approach to organizational development and organizational culture as an essential component of quality. Snyder is the coauthor, with Karolyn Snyder and Michele Acker-Hocevar, of *Living on the Edge of Chaos: Leading Schools into the Global Age* (2000; 2008), which has been translated into Chinese (2011), and coeditor of *Systems Thinking for Sustainable Schooling: A Mindshift for Educators to Lead and Achieve Quality in Schools* (2023). She has also authored *The Rainbow Runners: A Sled Dog Adventure*, which is a book about leadership and self-organizing teams.

Karolyn J. Snyder, EdD has served in education for over 50 years as a teacher, school leader, professor, and president of the International School Connection, Inc. With over 320 publications and professional work in 40 countries, her work has been grounded in a Systems Approach to school development, as well as newer developments in physics that offer guidance for leading school change over time. Over the last three decades, Snyder has also worked with school districts and universities around the world to strengthen the preparation of students as competent and caring global citizens. She is the developer of the Managing Productive Schools Training Program, which was the first systems approach model used to train educational leaders in the United States. In response to globalization and sustainable development, she developed the follow-up program, Leadership for Sustainable School Development. Snyder is also the author of the School Work Culture Profile (SWCP) diagnostic tool, which has been used internationally to help schools develop internal work systems that promote continuous improvement and responsiveness. Snyder is the coauthor of several books, including *Living on the Edge of Chaos: Leading Schools into the Global Age* (2000; 2008), with Kristen Snyder and Michele Acker-Hocevar, which has been translated into Chinese (2011); *Managing Productive Schools: Toward an Ecology* (1986) and *Competency Development for Managing Productive Schools* (1988), both with Robert H. Anderson. She has edited *Systems Thinking for Sustainable Schooling: A Mindshift for Educators to Lead and Achieve Quality in Schools* (2023) with Kristen Snyder, and *Clinical Supervision: Coaching for Higher Performance* with Robert H. Anderson (1993).

* * *

Dr. Michele Acker-Hocevar, PhD, Professor Emeritus of Washington State University (WSU), is a scholar of organizational behavior and theory. Her career spans over 45 years in public school teaching and administration, university teaching, and administration, culminating as Vice Chancellor of Academic Affairs. She was an editor of the *International Journal of Leadership in Education* (IJLE) and co-leader of a national study of school superintendents and principals sponsored by the University Council of Educational Administration.

Dr. Tammy Berryhill earned a bachelor's degree in Elementary Education, a master's degree in Educational Leadership, and a PhD in School Leadership. She has worked for 27 years in public schools as a teacher, assistant principal, principal, and assistant superintendent of schools. Currently, Dr. Berryhill is an elementary school principal. Her research interest and dissertation topic is titled Factors Impacting Elementary Principal Retention: Job Satisfaction, School Context, and Autonomous Decision-Making.

Dr. John Fitzgerald has worked as a teacher, consultant, principal, district supervisor, and superintendent with three Ontario School Districts in Canada. He has designed and coordinated the Principal's Qualification Program at the University of Ottawa. For 37 years, he was an instructor and instructor trainer with Performance Learning Systems (PLS) and served as an adjunct graduate professor at Drake University in Iowa and Leslie College in Massachusetts. He also served as Vice-President for Development and Co-Chair of the Board of Directors for the International School Connection (ISC).

Irmeli Halinen has influenced the development of the Finnish education system at school, municipal, and national levels since 1973. She has served as a curriculum expert for other countries and for the EU, OECD, and UNESCO. She was the Head of National Curriculum Development at the Finnish National Agency for Education and the main coordinator of the extensive curriculum reform in 2012–2016. She was a member of the Finnish National Commission for UNESCO, the National Evaluation Council of Education in Finland, and an expert member of the Advisory Board of the Finnish Ombudsman for Children. She retired from her permanent job in the autumn of 2016 and is now working as an author and international curriculum expert.

Dr. Helen M. Hazi is a Professor Emerita of Educational Leadership at West Virginia University. Her roots are in the "east coast" version of clinical supervision under Morris Cogan and Noreen Garman, which she returns to in her chapter. She has been a teacher, a Supervisor of Curriculum and Instruction, and an expert witness. She writes about legal issues that have consequences for teacher evaluation and instructional supervision in books and journals such as the *Journal of Educational Supervision* and *Teachers and Teaching: Theory and Practice*.

Dr. John Mann is a Senior Anchin Center Project Director for Leadership Development and Retired Instructor of Educational Leadership and Policy Studies at the University of South Florida. His long career has included the Principalship, Director of Leadership Development, and Assistant Superintendent of Curriculum and Instructional Services in Pasco County School District, Florida, in the United States. He has presented over 100 leadership training events and keynote addresses. John is most proud of his research focus on Appreciative Inquiry and Appreciative Organizing in Public Schools, as it applies to developing positive and sustainable organizations.

Dr. David Scanga has been an active educator for over 40 years. His public and international education career includes roles in school psychology, school and district leadership, and teaching leadership courses at Saint Leo University. Dr. David Scanga earned a bachelor's degree in Psychology, a master's degree in Educational Psychology, and a doctorate in Educational Leadership and Policy Studies.

Dr. Renee Sedlack has a doctorate degree in Educational Leadership and Policy Studies. For 41 years, she served as a teacher, assistant principal, principal, and human resources director. Dr. Sedlack is an Associate Professor of

Educational Leadership at Saint Leo University. Her research interest is in discovering ways to close the achievement gap among underserved youth.

Claudia Steinacker earned a bachelor's degree in Elementary Education, a master's degree in educational leadership, and an Education Specialist degree in Educational Leadership. She has worked for 26 years in public schools as a teacher, assistant principal, and principal. Her research interest is in exploring initiatives to ensure the success of young school leaders. Mrs. Steinacker is currently an elementary school principal.

Dr. Elaine Sullivan, a 38-year public school leader in Florida, was recognized as the U.S. 1998 National High School Principal of the Year and the 1997 Florida Principal of the Year. Sullivan created ISC youth initiatives and chaired the ISC Global Benchmark and Global Learning Center Programs. Dr. Sullivan developed the Quantum Strategic School Leadership Model.

www.ingramcontent.com/pod-product-compliance
Lightning Source LLC
Chambersburg PA
CBHW022015300426
44117CB00005B/198